COLONIAL
SPIRITS

COLONIAL SPIRITS

A Toast to Our Drunken History

BEING:
A Revolutionary Drinking Guide to
Brewing and Batching, Mixing and Serving,
Imbibing and Jibing, Fighting and Freedom
in the Ruins of the Ancient Civilization
Known as America

By Steven Grasse

ABRAMS IMAGE, NEW YORK

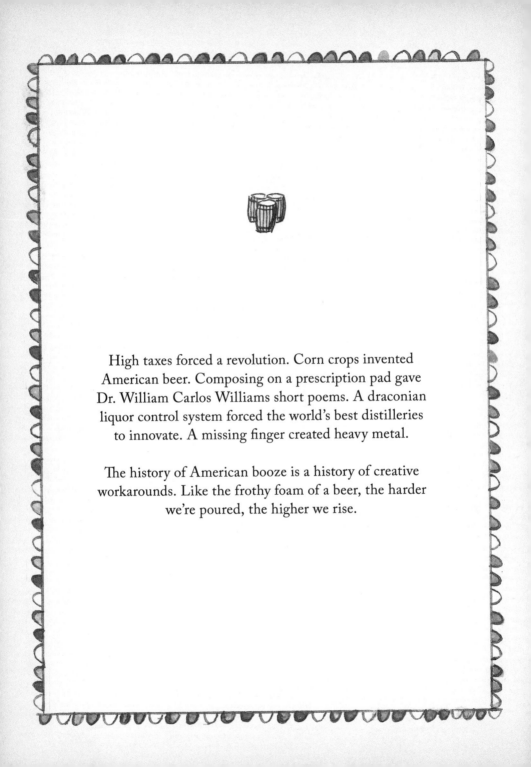

High taxes forced a revolution. Corn crops invented American beer. Composing on a prescription pad gave Dr. William Carlos Williams short poems. A draconian liquor control system forced the world's best distilleries to innovate. A missing finger created heavy metal.

The history of American booze is a history of creative workarounds. Like the frothy foam of a beer, the harder we're poured, the higher we rise.

✕✕ ✕✕✕✕ *CONTENTS* ✕✕✕✕✕✕

PROCLAMATION.

SPIRITS CAN BE MANY THINGS:
a transcendental search, the embodiment of inspiration, a
ghost in the closet, a bottle of booze.

We see the spirit of America as all of the above.

Before Democracy, there were spirits, and from spirits we
created taverns, and it was in those taverns that
we laid out the blueprint for a new kind of country,
with a new kind of ideology, not ruled
by kings and queens but by men and women.

In other words, we got drunk
and invented America.

Chapter I

Colonial Imbibing

OVERTURE

In the drink, a dream; and in the dream, a spark. So it has gone for more of American life and myth and invention than any teetotaler would ever admit. As children, for generations we have been given a version of our history that leans toward the puritanical. And it has gotten us into nothing but trouble. As a result, so many of us in this land—those of us who are lost equal to those of us who've never strayed—have grown up in battle, in endless war, pitting what we've been told versus what we know to be true: Morning in America has only been a result of nighttime in America.

And we have only been coming out of that night. If you visit Independence Hall, where our forefathers contentiously hammered out not just how we'd differentiate from British rule, not just how we'd win the war to have the right to do so, but also the very style of governance that guides us today, you will see (among other things) a chair. Cut in deep mahogany with a rich leather seat and gorgeous rails up the back that lead to a carving at the head, it is referred to as the Rising Sun Chair. This was the chair George

Washington himself sat in for months on end as the early American political power structure argued bitterly about what our version of democratic rule would look like. At the chair's head, one glimpses half of a golden sun, its brow and eyes and nose watching over what transpired there at Fifth and Chestnut Streets so many years ago. When all was said and done at that first Federal Convention of 1787, when our path was finally agreed to and set, Benjamin Franklin was heard to say perhaps the most American thing anyone has ever said: "I have often looked at that behind the president without being able to tell whether it was rising or setting. But now I know that it is a rising sun."

This book is a salute to those nights—nights of our forefathers putting to paper the rights we hold ever more dearly, nights that have given us freedom itself. Nights in a shed conjuring the modern world: Edison, flight, rock 'n' roll. Nights we thought we might not ever make it through. Nights made magnificent by the promise of the day to come.

Drinking, as it happens, is mostly done at night.

Our Method.

A Note on Our Methodology

The recipes you will enjoy in this humble tome are the result of diligent research and fearless testing. Our research team has delved into several centuries' worth of recipes culled from cookbooks of the period, historical record, anecdote, and folklore. We wanted to know not just what our American ancestors drank, but also why they drank it and how it was made.

What we found, time and time again, were two distinct facts:

- The early Americans tried to make booze from literally anything they could get their hands on. (See our notes on liquor from wood, page 154.)
- In relating these recipes to you, and updating them for modern times, it was of the utmost importance to us that you—yes, you—would not die or even be hospitalized should you choose to make or imbibe them.

And so we set out upon our noble effort to make the past come alive inside your mouth. But before we even started narrowing down our selections, we knew that we wanted these recipes to be so user-friendly that anyone with a can-do spirit and access to both the Internet and a local market could approximate them. Wherever possible, we have endeavored to share with you recipes that give the flavor and spirit of the originals without an overly arduous commitment of time or labor. We've also taken steps to ensure that many of the recipes bear a waste-not-want-not approach. (Didn't like your Cock Ale, for instance? Well, at the very least, you are now in possession of a mighty fine soup stock.) That resourceful, DIY spirit is central not just to our own philosophy but also to the early American spirit, which we know you'll find as refreshing as we did. It is our finest hope that this book honors past, present, and future Americans alike. It no doubt will also offer all of them a stiff drink.

With recipes in hand, our crack team of chefs, mixologists, and tasters alike entered the test kitchen, where we honed the recipes you see before you. There was trial; there was error; and then there were more of both; and finally, there was success. Once a recipe passed muster (and with no less than a dozen tasters, this was no mean feat), it was then laid out more or less as you see it before you. However, our work was then tested once more by our publisher, who made sure all these recipes adhere to widely acknowledged and regulated standards of things that can be safely ingested by the human body.

These drinks may get you drunk. They may put hair on your chest. They may send a surge of history-lightning through your organism. But they will not, we are proud to say with some measure of confidence, kill you.

Drink up. It's later than you think.

COMING TO AMERICA:
SOME NOTES ON THE PILGRIMS

It is not generally known that, among the earliest American settlers, Pilgrims—those descendants of English Puritanism whose strange and frankly quite often wrong ideas about human life (see John Robinson's edict that women are "the weaker vessel"; we're still trying to clean up from that one)—made up only 40 percent of those who were coming over here. Who were the other 60 percent? They were unskilled laborers and skilled workers alike, merchants and craftsmen, indentured servants, and the otherwise indigent people who'd somehow scrapped and scraped their way onto the boat. And even among this motley, random lot, don't think these so-called Pilgrims were in any kind of consensus. In a feat of cognitive dissonance that would set the tone for American politics to this day, the Puritans had the nerve to call them "strangers." Not shipmates, not colleagues, not even—oddly—friends.

It is in the name of those "strangers" that we'd like to point out the following today and for all time: No, no, it was not for religious freedom nor by divine providence that our ancestors so fatefully settled at Plymouth Rock. It was because we were running out of beer.

But even a cursory read of history will tell you the Pilgrims weren't the first European settlers in America; they merely had the best press.

In fact, from the moment John Cabot discovered Newfoundland in 1497, a slow trickle of Europeans had begun to settle in what would later become Virginia and New England. Sent by merchant companies to extract gold, oil, wine, and silk to export back to the Continent, these early outliers and "strangers" illustrate an important point that we must always keep in mind about this country: At any given moment in America's development, we were only one whim of the Crown away from being designated a penal colony à la Australia. For our truest spiritual roots are not those of piety and solemnity; they are those of castoffs, freaks, scrappers. Populations we would deem today as being "at risk."

Take, for example, John Smith, whose tale exemplifies America's rascal youth. This explorer and soldier gets his proper due as perhaps being the man who did more than any single other person to outline the territories that would become Jamestown and New England. But this achievement is merely the pull quote in a lifetime highlights reel that saw him variously as a swashbuckler, a slave, apparently a rather formidable lover (his mistress fell in love with him), an escapee, a mutineer, and so on. Smith's life, at least in his own estimation, was a one-man adventure novel, and it sets the stage for a kind of American exceptionalism that to this day begins in the imagination (and often stays there).

In the most famous (and very likely completely apocryphal) lore about Smith, he's an accidental diplomat, which he becomes when Pocahontas

famously takes a shine to his charms just as her tribesmen are about to beat him to a bloody pulp. True or not, Smith's escapades and the goodwill they generated between natives and settlers would benefit the Pilgrims years down the line. The Native Americans would teach the Plymouth Rock settlers, struggling to survive in a new land, how to ferment alcohol from corn; in some corners, even this was construed as a tribute to Smith and his legend.

But wait, you're saying, they were Pilgrims: Did not their Puritan ways of piety and seriousness look askance at the consumption of alcoholic beverages? Why would they drink?

Because they were afraid of the water.

WATER, WATER, EVERYWHERE BUT NOT A DROP TO DRINK

Let us begin with an experiment. Imagine every glass of water you drink in a day, the jump cut of when you first awake, then on to breakfast, then at work, next at lunch, and onward through the day. Finally, reimagine all that, in the exact same detail except for one: That's not water—it's beer.

Good morning, Early American you. Then as now and as in the future, water loomed as both a danger and a dream for all men and women on earth. In the 1600s, when man still had little grasp of what we today hold as the basics of science, there was little concept of water purification. Instead, water putrefaction ruled the day, and often, to drink a glass of water was to take your life into your own hands.

Water—dirty, filthy, stinking, rotten water—was but one of a myriad of motivations for our American ancestors to quit the European scene. (Not just the physical space of Britain and Europe, but also its fiscal and spiritual constraints.) But for our purposes here, let us dwell for a moment primarily on the physical repercussions of England's and Europe's very dangerous and quite bad . . . water.

The Enlightenment (and all that came before it) be damned, Brits and Europeans alike made no progress in waterways and sanitation from where the Romans left off—in fact, they did notably worse. Having ignored ancient Rome's signature contribution to humanity—devising ways to deliver clean water to human beings—the waterways of the old countries, from London straight through eastern Europe, were literal cesspools, and would remain so up through the eighteenth century.

Until then, your average person would know most waterways, be they rivers or sewers, as being loaded with bacteria and waste. And not just the environmentally unfriendly offloading by corporate rogues we know today: No, the seventeenth-century system of pollution was so, well, systemic that no one even thought of it as pollution. It was simply what you did with your human waste, your animal waste, your garbage, perhaps, say, any old blood you had lying around—you simply chucked it into the Thames! London's notable diversion from this nasty habit was an early form of recycling that would ring ironic with any backyard composter today: At the end of each day, the City of London employed wagons to go around and collect the waste from public outhouses. From there, it would be deposited outside the city in a series of nitrate beds, where they'd make the only thing they could think to make with old shit in those days: gunpowder.

No wonder, then, that given a choice of something to drink—any choice at all, really—your average Briton and Continental alike would eschew drinking water entirely. This had been the case, as far as we can tell, since

the Middle Ages. (And indeed, clean drinking water would elude England altogether until well into the nineteenth century, when a lurching green stink so enveloped the Thames that one could smell it and in fact be sickened from it in the very chambers of Parliament.) As a result, a common folk wisdom would arise during these times declaring that not only was booze a much safer potable than water, it was, in fact, overwhelmingly good for you, loaded with nutrients, and beneficial to your health and your humors. And it was more than folk wisdom: As alchemy gave way to the apothecary, a patient would be prescribed herb- and botanical-infused liquors for any number of ailments. In an age just before we knew of bacteria and viruses, "ill humors" and "miasmas" alike had a way of being around (bad, filthy, nasty) water. This was less so the case with booze, so in this haphazard fashion, booze became a cure as well as a preventive measure. Water, they'd say: It's enough to make you drink!

Throughout the 1600s, the American settlers began to arrive. First, they came in smaller numbers. But by the end of the century, a quantifiable wave of emigrants was in evidence. And among them, there was a sizable portion who'd slowly but surely come to demand independence with a clear-eyed will to forge a new land free from the religious and class

structures (including the taxation without representation) that stifled the old one. And when they got here, they were understandably astonished to find clean, clear water in great abundance. All over the colonies, from the streams of New England to the rivers of Pennsylvania and on down to the Chesapeake Bay, our American ancestors universally cheered what they regarded as a novelty so exotic they didn't quite know what to do with it: clean water. And so they began to do with it what they did in the old country: dump every manner of waste into it. Science concerning the eradication of bacteria, such as that proved by someone like Louis Pasteur, wouldn't be around for another two hundred years or so, and besides, it's like they always say: Old habits die hard. Back to the booze it was, then.

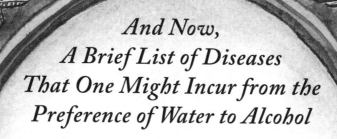

And Now,
A Brief List of Diseases
That One Might Incur from the
Preference of Water to Alcohol

smallpox • dengue fever • influenza • black vomit
• lockjaw • crib death • bloody flux • scowring •
canker and thrush • dropsy • French pox • green sickness
• griping in the guts • "king's evil" • lethargy • pleurisy •
rickets • "rising of the lights" • sores • ulcers • sadness

As you may imagine, for the fearless or desperate soul who'd dare consume the vile waters of the 1600s, there was often hell to pay. Among them, say, "king's evil," or scrofula, an infection of the lymph nodes that would cause chronic cold abscesses, which also could be a prime indicator that you were well on your way to tuberculosis. Its cure? Well, there was something called the "royal touch" or the "king's touch," in which the sufferer would be lucky enough to enjoy a laying on of hands by a documented royal. In addition to the difficulties involved in actually getting one's wretched body in front of a willing member of the royalty, this treatment did not work, because none of this is science.

HERE memory's spell wakes up
the trong of paft affection;
HERE our fathers trod.

—William Penn addressing his fellow drinkers at the Blue Anchor, 1682

BEHOLD, AMERICA DRINKS!

All of America, all that we know in our bones as citizens, our folkways, our friendliness, and spirit of trade and fair play and hard play alike, stems not from our churches but from our bars. And yet, perhaps thanks to Puritanism still having its way with us hundreds of years after its sell-by date, this simple fact is missing but essential to our understanding of American history. Nevertheless, there it is.

In so many ways, America is a bar: open to everyone, available to whoever can afford it, and apparently quite difficult to get kicked out of. And if that's true, it is a big bar, with rooms upon rooms, one clientele sharing quarters, stacked, with other clienteles. So much so that in America's earliest days, the streets of the small but rapidly growing towns and cities would be connected, block by block and family to family, by bars. A popular wisdom of the colonial age went thus: Americans would spend 50 pounds to erect a church and 400 pounds to erect a tavern.

And as Samuel Cole's life story illustrates, no sooner did our forefathers tread upon this soil than they were brewing beer and building taverns.

Guy Walks into a Bar: The Sad but True Tale of America's First Pubkeeper

Consider, if you will, the humble barkeep, and everything that we know about him or her today. The good ones among the tribe are, without fail, good listeners; built of a robust constitution that the occupation, night in and night out, demands; they breach no discretion, levy no judgment, and take nothing that is not freely offered. And yet, there is an attendant journeyman darkness that marks them: failed marriages, false starts, stories untold and washed away in the endless tide of the patron's gab.

Samuel Cole knew that color. After arriving in Boston in 1630, Cole was granted the first tavern license in all of New England in 1634. (Although it was not, it must be noted, first in the colonies as a whole: The tavern bearing that honor was in Jamestown some years prior. Sadly, however, scant information about the place made the leap into historical record.) His venue quickly became the center of social and political life in Boston, so much so that Cole himself would drift into political life for a time. At the tavern, governors and lords and Indian chiefs alike would break bread, thereby establishing a thread that would persist through American colonial life—the tavern as the very center of all social activities, both official and nonofficial.

But beware the barman who talks politics: At the height of his prosperity, Cole found himself on the losing end of a politico-religious schism and would wind up dying a pauper. (His descendants, though they would know successes in this land of freedom, would never get the brass ring. None other than Abraham Lincoln would pass one of Cole's great-grandchildren over for the presidency; still another, generations later and in a time of diminished expectations, would be cut off by a man called Mitt Romney.)

In literature, however, Samuel Cole would achieve immortality, thanks to one of his own regulars, Henry Wadsworth Longfellow. The poet and playwright dropped Cole, name and all, into his play *John Endicott*, in what might have been the first portrayal of an American tavern keeper in our entire national literature. In *John Endicott*, Cole appears as prideful of his public house, inviting and magnanimous. In real life, Cole's pub was called Cole's Inn. But Longfellow dubbed it the Three Mariners.

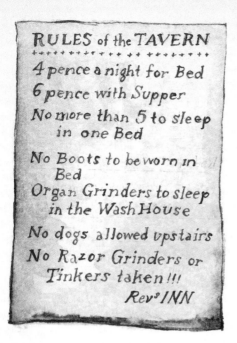

RULES of the TAVERN
+·+·+·++·+·+·++·+·++·+·++·+·+·++

4 pence a night for Bed

6 pence with Supper

No more than 5 to sleep
in one Bed

No Boots to be worn in
Bed

Organ Grinders to sleep
in the Wash House

No dogs allowed upstairs

No Razor Grinders or
Tinkers taken !!!

Rev⁵ INN

In 1682, William Penn landed at the Blue Anchor, a tavern in what is now Philadelphia's Society Hill area (which is also, by the way, the neighborhood from whence we address you today, dear reader). The Blue Anchor doubled as a boat landing, thanks to its position on Dock Creek, a small (now buried) tributary just steps from the Delaware River. Think of it as a precursor to your favorite river deck bar, only it was also a hotel, a court, a trading post, a post office, and more—as was every tavern in those days. By every account, the Blue Anchor was—in its first incarnation, anyway—first rate, a key to the city itself. (Like most bars, it would change hands and clientele often.) And as Penn took his first steps on Philadelphia soil, his first visit to an American bar would be the stuff of history:

"The whole scene was active, animating and cheering. On the shore were gathered, to cheer his arrival, most of the few inhabitants who had preceded him. He was naturally prone to cheerfulness for a grave public friend, especially in the eyes of those who held religion harsh, intolerant, austere."

—*Watson's Annals of Philadelphia & Pennsylvania*, c. 1830–1850

The party, as he would eventually lament later in life, had started without him. As directed by county officials, acting upon the orders of the Crown, taverns were quickly erected in every community to serve all the purposes (and more) one could partake of at the Blue Anchor. In the absence of anywhere else that hosted those essential functions, tavern keepers were, as you might imagine, among the wealthiest personages in the community. And in the days before a proper American currency was established, the tavern was often a bank of sorts as well—beer would be used as a currency or item of barter (and so it went for tobacco as well). In lieu of pay, militiamen were attracted to their drills by the promise of free ale. This, of course, was so popular that drills quickly became riotous affairs and a precursor to a rising hooliganism that would plague both colonial and free America well into the 1800s. Hand in hand with that hooliganism would be this uncomfortable fact: Those hooligans were among the first to demand America's independence from British rule.

The irony of it all? Taverns first mandated by the Crown would be later used for purposes of sedition. In blithely demanding that America tavernize itself, the king ultimately sowed the seeds of his own doom. Taverns would come to serve the resistance more than they served the Crown, performing all the functions once set forth by the king and then some—only instead for the revolutionary side. This, of course, set the stage for the long American tradition of people hatching plans in bars, a natural birthright of the American tribe that persists to this day.

In Philadelphia alone, taverns produced themselves at a dizzying rate. There was the Blue Anchor, the Penny Pot Tavern, Tun Tavern, the Edinburgh Brewhouse (run by Mary Lisle, the Betsy Ross of beer), the still-standing Man Full of Trouble (proprietor: Martha Smallwood), and scores of others. By 1776, there would be more than one hundred licensed taverns in the small walkable area that is now Philadelphia's Old City and Society Hill sections—roughly one square mile. Together, the taverns would account for no less than 10 percent of all then-extant Philadelphia real estate. (And among those, one-fifth would be run by women.) Meanwhile, there were also "private tippling houses"—early speakeasies, if you will—leading a shadow economy, to be ferreted out by grand juries.

Embargoes from our soon-to-be-cast-off overlords across the sea, as well as a general desire on the part of these new Americans to mint new folkways and traditions, led directly to the very thing this book is about: our forefathers making booze out of pretty much anything they could get their hands on.

But in the beginning, there was beer.

A MAP OF THE
APPROXIMATE LOCATIONS
OF PHILADELPHIA'S TAVERNS,
PUBS, AND TIPPLING HOUSES

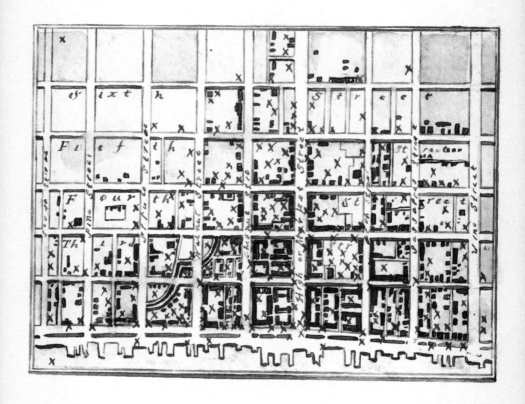

CHAPTER II

Beer

BREWERS WANTED

We live in a time in which beer is ubiquitous. Never before have we been able to enjoy so vast a variety of beers and ales begotten by such a variety of brewers and providers, be they macro- or microbrews, or even the single batch whipped up by you and your neighbors, the humble hobbyists. But for the bloody, desperate, and glorious three hundred years of Americans before us, a wholly different age of ubiquitous beer prevailed. Although there were different varieties in evidence in every hill and dell—Beers we can't but imagine! Beers we will never know! Beers we will, by God, show you how to make here today!—"ubiquitous beer" in colonial times was ubiquitous in that man, woman, and, yes, even child drank it all the livelong goddamned day.

No sooner did we tread upon American soil in the early 1600s than what has turned into our never-ending quest for never-ending beer began. And immediately it became apparent that the settlers would have to make do with what was on hand. At Plymouth Rock, the Wampanoags taught them how to ferment alcohol, but of what use was that alone, really, if you've nothing to ferment?

Whoever drinks beer, he is quick to sleep; whoever does not sin, enters Heaven! Thus, let us drink beer!

—Martin Luther

For beer is made this way, if you didn't know: First, you need a grain (most often barley, yes, but really, any old grain will do) and you need to malt that grain, only to then make a hot mash out of it. Then boil it with hops and allow the resulting "wort" to cool; strain the wort and ferment it with yeast. Next, you wait. And then you have beer.

But there was a wrench in the works for our earliest American brewers: a distinct lack of hops. Some lucky settlers did manage to find hops growing in the wild, but their supply was quickly exhausted, leaving them in the same awful situation they were in when they were dropped off by mercenary sail-

ors here in the first place: There just wasn't enough beer to go around. Like a college party, once the crew on the *Mayflower* saw that they were down to their last few barrels of ale, they cleared the ship. Heavy friends only would partake for the duration.

In Jamestown, Virginia, the situation was even worse: Somehow, the early settlers there had managed to come all the way over to the colony without thinking to bring someone who actually knew how to make beer. After knocking on every door to see if any of the settlers ever knew, or could remember, could maybe just get lucky and figure out how beer was made, they took the only option left to them: In 1609, they wrote back to London and placed ads in the local papers seeking a brewer, any brewer at all. Imag-ine the hero's welcome that hearty soul received when at long last he stepped off the boat and into the grateful arms of the people of Jamestown.

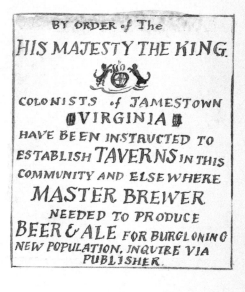

BY ORDER of The
HIS MAJESTY THE KING.

COLONISTS of JAMESTOWN
VIRGINIA
HAVE BEEN INSTRUCTED TO
ESTABLISH TAVERNS IN THIS
COMMUNITY AND ELSEWHERE
MASTER BREWER
NEEDED TO PRODUCE
BEER & ALE FOR BURGLONING
NEW POPULATION. INQUIRE VIA
PUBLISHER.

Our desire for beer was, as discussed, both a born-in cultural habit as well as what was then a common-sense approach not to drink water and possibly die in any one of a myriad of unappeal-ing ways. What the settlers could not have expected was that this appetite would not immediately be sated in what was both a boun-teous and confoundingly harsh new land.

And so it was that improvisation prevailed. As one would expect, prior to the advent of taverns in America, all beer was brewed at home—there was nowhere else to do it. And in point of fact, even by the mid-1700s, when tav-erns lined early American streets, "private tippling houses" were still in such abundance that grand juries existed in each of the larger cities for the express purpose of ferreting them out. Speakeasies, it turned out, were in our DNA. And it would take hundreds of years for them to be beaten out of us. But that is a story for another time.

SMALL BEER

As the early Americans broadened their efforts to accrue the variety of beers, ales, and ciders they had enjoyed across the Atlantic, so too did the old social pecking order of drinks begin to manifest itself. Working men enjoyed the strongest ales; Quakers, whose teetotaling has been somewhat exaggerated by history, took cider; women and children drank something called small beer, which was itself a sort of "base beer"—small beer being the simplest beer one could make. Brewed and fermented for a much shorter time than proper beers and ales, small beer bore a lower alcohol level and not as strong a flavor. It would, to modern tastes, register as sour—but then, so would all beers of this pre-pasteurization era.

GENERAL GEORGE WASHINGTON'S SMALL BEER

To Make Small Beer

Take a large Siffer [Sifter] full of Bran Hops to your Taste. —Boil these 3 hours. Then strain out 30 Gall[ons] into a cooler, put in 3 Gall[ons] Molasses while the Beer is Scalding hot or rather draw the Molasses into the cooler & St[r]ain the Beer on it while boiling Hot. Let this stand till it is little more than Blood warm. Then put in a quart of Yea[s]t if the Weather is very Cold, cover it over with a Blank[et] & let it Work in the Cooler 24 hours then put it into the Cask—leave the bung open till it is almost don[e] Working— Bottle it that Week it was Brewed.

—From a notebook (c. 1757) kept by George Washington

Stock Ale

OUR RECIPE

MAKES 1 GALLON (3.8 L)

Our goal here was to re-create a Colonial era–inspired beer that would be an exceptional brown ale in all the recipes contained in this book calling for brown ale. For the beginner brewer, take this recipe to your nearest home-brew store for assistance and assemble the ingredients and necessary equipment. Searching "home-brew supplies" online will also provide plenty of resources to help you get started. We were able to procure everything we needed to brew a gallon of Stock Ale for less than a hundred dollars.

For your reference: *Wort* is the term for unfermented beer. *Trub* is the term for the sludge that settles on the bottom of the stockpot or fermenter. Sanitation is extremely important when brewing. Your home-brew store will be able to set you up with proper sanitizing procedures.

Supplies:

Stainless steel stockpot
2-gallon (7.5-L) fermenting bucket with
   stopper, air lock, and spigot (this doubles
   as the bottling bucket)
Cheesecloth sack
Kitchen thermometer with a register of at
   least 40° to 180°F (4 to 82°C)
Stainless steel stirring spoon

Siphon
Carboy
Bottle filler
12 (12-ounce / 360-ml) bottles
Bottle caps and capper
Carb tabs

continued

Ingredients:

1½ gallons (5.8 L) filtered water
2 pounds (910 g) Maris Otter malt
1 cup (225 g) amber malt
1 ounce (30 g) Kent Goldings Hops

½ cup (120 ml) molasses for baking
1 packet (0.4 ounces/11.5 g) Safbrew S-33 yeast

Sanitize all equipment prior to beginning.

- In a large stockpot, bring the water to 170°F (75°C). Meanwhile, put the Maris Otter malt and amber malt in a cheesecloth sack, and make a knot in the sack to tie off.

- Submerge the sack of malt in the hot water and steep for 2 hours, maintaining a constant temperature of 150° to 155°F (65° to 70°C). Keep an eye on the temperature the entire time—a kettle of boiling water and an alternate container of cool water are useful to have on hand to keep the brew at the correct temperature.

- After 2 hours, remove the sack of malt and transfer it to a large bowl. These grains can be discarded—or, once they have cooled, measure them out by the cup and freeze for future baking projects.

- Add ¾ ounce (20 g) of the Kent Goldings hops to the wort and bring to a rapid boil. Boil for 45 minutes.

- Add the molasses and boil for 15 minutes more.

- Turn off the heat, add the remaining ¼ ounce (10 g) of Kent Goldings hops, and cover.

- Submerge the pot in an ice bath (a kitchen sink works well for this) and chill until the brew reaches 70°F (20°C).

- Siphon the wort into a fermenting bucket, leaving any trub in the bottom of the stockpot.

- Add the yeast to the wort, snap on the lid, and place the fermenting bucket in a room-temperature area that will not be disturbed.

- Seal the bucket with a stopper and air lock.

- Allow the wort to ferment for 2 to 3 days at room temperature.

- Remove the stopper and air lock. Siphon the fermenting wort into a sanitized glass carboy, leaving any trub in the fermenting bucket. Seal the carboy with a stopper and air lock and ferment for another 7 to 10 days.

- Once the wort has fermented a second time, it is ready to bottle. Assemble and sanitize the bottles, bottle caps, siphon, bottle filler, and bottling bucket. Siphon the wort from the carboy into the bottling bucket, keeping any trub left in the carboy.

- Add 3 to 4 carb tabs to each empty bottle.

- Attach the siphon and bottle filler to the bucket spigot. Open the spigot, fill, and cap the bottles.

- Store the bottled beer at room temperature, away from light, for 1 to 3 weeks before serving.

TAVERNISM

Around the world and throughout history, it is ever true and 'twas ever thus: Humans begat beer, and beer begat taverns. But walk into any bar in America, be it in Cheboygan or Chicago or Charlotte, and you will feel a distant echo of the American colonial tavern moment and its true, unimpeachable populism. And that populism is about what we drank as well as where we drank it. You, Mr. or Ms. Urban Beer Snob, may find your uncle's favorite macrobrew or your cousin's oh-so-precious local beer reprehensible on any number of levels. But even within that scope of commercial offerings, you can also find the contours of the American dream. These are beers produced for everyone, shipped wholesale to bars where, for the most part, everyone is welcome to drink them. Teenagers who know nothing will drink them; so too will grizzled academics who know that everything is nothing anyway. Criminals will know their flavor profiles, as will presidents.

And in these potions, we see a faint glimmer of our nonexclusive history. Before America had been bought and sold so many times over, before corporations were people, and before people were therefore stripped of their own status as people, there was a bar. You remember it; that's right! It was a bar called America! And you could do everything you needed to do there.

In fact, there were (and thus, we are made of) hundreds and hundreds of bars called America. Each of them bore a personality as different as each face in every crowd. And over time, a visual vernacular developed in the taverns' signage that was designed to show you that face. Above, we show you a selection of those beautiful faces, the signs that declared their presence and goodwill to all passersby, re-created from historical record, in our own hand.

AN APPEAL TO HEAVEN

Dear Friend: I write to you today just blocks from the Betsy Ross House, where each day visitors are given a scrubbed-up version of history that denies them some of the most basic truths about who we are and where we came from. One truth is that this place was not even Betsy Ross's house. Another truth is that it was not she who single-handedly designed and produced the American flag. It is still another truth that her name was not even Betsy Ross. Moreover, here is the truest truth we know: History is chaos. And the American flag that is today loved and loathed and elevated and desecrated all over the world could have just as easily been a white flag bearing nothing but the image of a pine tree and the simple inscription, "An Appeal to Heaven."

In fact, it almost was.

Like the stars and stripes and the "Don't Tread on Me" flag and who knows how many other iterations of flags before it, "An Appeal to Heaven" was borne of a confluence of ideas that met in the right place at the right time. From the early 1600s, explorers of the colonies were struck by the preponderance of pine and spruce trees on the East Coast, especially in New England. These trees instantly became a valuable resource and a symbol of the freedom and opportunity the New World promised. The trees produced a fine timber for shipbuilding, and in a pinch, their needles could also be used for—what else?—beer.

Meanwhile, merchant ships and militias alike adopted the pine as a talisman; by the 1770s, both George Washington's Continental Army and the Massachusetts State Navy were flying the flag. The pine, of course, stood as a symbol of the land; the legend, "An Appeal to Heaven," referenced what was by then a widely held idea that American independence was nothing less than a divine right. John Locke, in his Treatise on Civil Government, first uttered the phrase; the idea being that in a world where governments (such as the Crown) would not hear an appeal for natural freedoms, the only place one could reasonably place such a request would be with the Man Upstairs himself. Locke's notion found itself in more than a flag; Thomas Jefferson would wind up borrowing freely from Locke in something called the Declaration of Independence. It's a great document about how awesome we used to be, and could be again someday.

SPRUCE BEER

Pine and spruce trees would eventually become the stuff of revolution, and it's not hard to see why. Beyond their simple majesty and abundance, the economic force wielded by their export was formidable. And the king had his misshapen paw in every last bit of it, on up until 1772, when his craven wish to harvest trees before their time led directly to the Pine Tree Riot. When colonials refused to pull down the trees, the king's army tried to go medieval, dishing out lashes, mutilating man and horse alike. Instead, the people rioted, advancing a cause that would presage the revolt eventually exhibited at the Boston Tea Party a few years later. It is to that rebel spirit that we dedicate this recipe for Spruce Beer, its prickly needles a symbol for the thousands who dared to make "An Appeal to Heaven."

SPRUCE BEER

To Brew Spruce Beer

Take four ounces of hops, let them boil half an hour in one gallon of water, strain the hop water then add sixteen gallons of warm water, two gallons of molasses, eight ounces of essence of spruce, dissolved in one quart of water, put in a clean cask, then shake it well together, add half a pint of emptins, then let it stand and work one week, if very warm weather less time will do, when it is drawn off to bottle, add one spoonful of molasses to every bottle.

—From *American Cookery* by Amelia Simmons, 1798

Spruce Ale

OUR RECIPE

The historic recipe calls for spruce essence to be added to hop water and molasses. Our approach is to add spruce essence to a brown ale. Premade spruce essence can be bought at home-brew shops, but we prefer to make our own.

Resources for spruce tips are rather limited. They can be found online through home-brew or herbal retailers. Often they are sold dried as a tea. For our version of Spruce Ale, we actually used dried Douglas fir tips with great results.

Fresh spruce tips can also be foraged in the spring. The green tips of new growth are needed to make spruce essence. If using fresh tips, start with about half the amount as dried. If the essence is too weak, remove the steeped tips and simmer again with more tips. If the essence is too strong, dilute with water once the essence has cooled.

Whatever you choose, remember that every tree is different, and no two spruce essences will be exactly the same. We recommend using this recipe as a mere starting point for experimentation with your own revolutionary imaginings.

NOTE: *If you decide to strike out on your own to collect the tips of the mighty spruce, beware. Not all evergreens are edible, and some (including yew, evergreen oleander, and holly) are toxic.*

Spruce Essence
MAKES 2 CUPS (480 ML)

1 ounce (28 g) dried spruce fir tips

⅛ teaspoon salt

- In a medium saucepan with a lid, combine the dried spruce/fir tips, salt, and 2 cups (480 ml) water. Bring to a boil and cover. Lower the heat and simmer, covered, for 30 minutes.
- Cool the mixture and then strain. Store in an airtight container in the refrigerator for up to 1 week.

Spruce Ale
SERVES 1

¼ cup (60 ml) spruce essence

1½ cups (360 ml) chilled brown ale or Stock Ale (see recipe, page 21)

Pour the spruce essence into a pint glass. Top with the ale and serve.

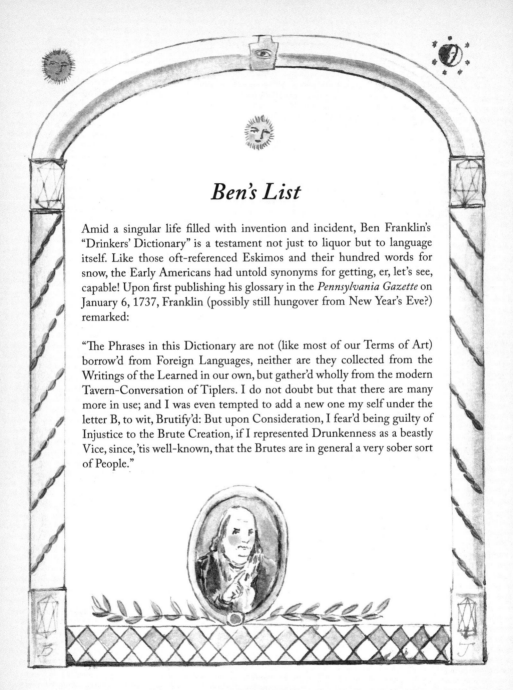

Ben's List

Amid a singular life filled with invention and incident, Ben Franklin's "Drinkers' Dictionary" is a testament not just to liquor but to language itself. Like those oft-referenced Eskimos and their hundred words for snow, the Early Americans had untold synonyms for getting, er, let's see, capable! Upon first publishing his glossary in the *Pennsylvania Gazette* on January 6, 1737, Franklin (possibly still hungover from New Year's Eve?) remarked:

"The Phrases in this Dictionary are not (like most of our Terms of Art) borrow'd from Foreign Languages, neither are they collected from the Writings of the Learned in our own, but gather'd wholly from the modern Tavern-Conversation of Tiplers. I do not doubt but that there are many more in use; and I was even tempted to add a new one my self under the letter B, to wit, Brutify'd: But upon Consideration, I fear'd being guilty of Injustice to the Brute Creation, if I represented Drunkenness as a beastly Vice, since, 'tis well-known, that the Brutes are in general a very sober sort of People."

A
He is Addled
He's casting up his
  Accounts
He's Afflicted
He's in his Airs

B
He's Biggy
Bewitch'd
Block and Block
Boozy
Bowz'd
Been at Barbadoes
Piss'd in the Brook
Drunk as a
  Wheel-Barrow
Burdock'd
Buskey
Buzzey
Has Stole a Manchet
  out of the
  Brewer's Basket
His Head is full of
  Bees
Has been in the
  Bibbing Plot
Has drank more
  than he has bled
He's Bungey
As Drunk as a
  Beggar
He sees the Bears
He's kiss'd black
  Betty
He's had a Thump
  over the Head
  with Sampson's
  Jawbone
He's Bridgey

C
He's Cat
Cagrin'd

Capable
Cramp'd
Cherubimical
Cherry Merry
Wamble Crop'd
Crack'd
Concern'd
Half Way to Concord
Has taken a
  Chirriping-Glass
Got Corns in his
  Head
A Cup too much
Coguy
Copey
He's heat his Copper
He's Crocus
Catch'd
He cuts his Capers
He's been in the
  Cellar
He's in his Cups
Non Compos
Cock'd
Curv'd
Cut
Chipper
Chickery
Loaded his Cart
He's been too free
  with the Creature
Sir Richard has
  taken off his
  Considering Cap
He's Chap-fallen

D
He's Disguiz'd
He's got a Dish
Kill'd his Dog
Took his Drops
It is a Dark Day
  with him
He's a Dead Man

Has Dipp'd his Bill
He's Dagg'd
He's seen the Devil

E
He's Prince Eugene
Enter'd
Wet both Eyes
Cock Ey'd
Got the Pole Evil
Got a brass Eye
Made an Example
He's Eat a Toad &
  half for Breakfast
In his Element

F
He's Fishey
Fox'd
Fuddled
Sore Footed
Frozen
Well in for't
Owes no Man a
  Farthing
Fears no Man
Crump Footed
Been to France
Flush'd
Froze his Mouth
Fetter'd
Been to a Funeral
His Flag is out
Fuzl'd
Spoke with his
  Friend
Been at an Indian
  Feast

G
He's Glad
Groatable
Gold-headed
Glaiz'd

Generous
Booz'd the Gage
As Dizzy as a Goose
Been before George
Got the Gout
Had a Kick in the
  Guts
Been with Sir John
  Goa
Been at Geneva
Globular
Got the Glanders

H
Half and Half
Hardy
Top Heavy
Got by the Head
Hiddey
Got on his little Hat
Hammerish
Loose in the Hilts
Knows not the way
  Home
Got the Hornson
Haunted with Evil
  Spirits
Has Taken
  Hippocrates'
  grand Elixir

I to J
He's Intoxicated
Jolly
Jagg'd
Jambled
Going to Jerusalem
Jocular
Been to Jerico
Juicy

K

He's a King
Clips the King's
  English
Seen the French
  King
The King is his
  Cousin
Got Kib'd Heels
Knapt
Het his Kettle

L

He's in Liquor
Lordly
He makes Indentures
  with his Leggs
Well to Live
Light
Lappy
Limber

M

He sees two Moons
Merry
Middling
Moon-Ey'd
Muddled
Seen a Flock of
  Moons
Maudlin
Mountous
Muddy
Rais'd his
  Monuments
Mellow

N

He's eat the
  Cocoa Nut

Nimptopsical
Got the Night Mare

O

He's Oil'd
Eat Opium
Smelt of an Onion
Oxycrocium
Overset

P

He drank till he
  gave up his
  Half-Penny
Pidgeon Ey'd
Pungey
Priddy
As good conditioned
  as a Puppy
Has scalt his
  Head Pan
Been among the
  Philistines
In his Prosperity
He's been among the
  Philippians
He's contending with
  Pharaoh
Wasted his Paunch
He's Polite
Eat a Pudding Bagg

Q

He's Quarrelsome

R

He's Rocky
Raddled
Rich
Religious

Lost his Rudder
Ragged
Rais'd
Been too free with
  Sir Richard
Like a Rat in
  Trouble

S

He's Stitch'd
Seafaring
In the Sudds
Strong
Been in the Sun
As Drunk as
  David's Sow
Swampt
His Skin is full
He's Steady
He's Stiff
He's burnt his
  Shoulder
He's got his Top
  Gallant Sails out
Seen the yellow Star
As Stiff as a
  Ring-bolt
Half Seas over
His Shoe pinches him
Staggerish
It is Star-light with
  him
He carries too much
  Sail
Stew'd
Stubb'd
Soak'd
Soft

Been too free
  with Sir John
  Strawberry
He's right before
  the Wind with
  all his Studding
  Sails out
Has Sold his Senses

T

He's Top'd
Tongue-ty'd
  Tann'd
Tipium Grove
Double Tongu'd
Topsy Turvey
Tipsey
Has Swallow'd a
  Tavern Token
He's Thaw'd
He's in a Trance
He's Trammel'd

V

He makes Virginia
  Fence
Valiant
Got the Indian
  Vapours

W

The Malt is above
  the Water
He's Wise
He's Wet
He's been to the Salt
  Water
He's Water-soaken
He's very Weary
Out of the Way

COCK ALE

The lusty nature of our forefathers is something that has been covered up to all but the most astute readers of history for far too long. But we can say it now, and with pride: On a scale from Grandma Moses on one end and the filthiest pirate on the other, our early American drinkers most often fell somewhere closest to, say, Charlie Sheen in a three-cornered hat. As we have discussed, they often drank all day, every day. But they did other things, too. Things like having sex and practicing DIY medicine. Cock Ale got both of these jobs done.

A mixture of ale and a boozy, spiced chicken broth, essentially, Cock Ale stands as an example of the prevailing wisdom of the time, which said that booze was indeed for health and vigor, as well as a cure for what ails you. In this case, Cock Ale also stands as perhaps America's first erectile dysfunction medication. Yes, really.

In the 1600s, as revolution began to permeate the air, so, too, did America's first coffee craze. Parallel to the colonies' rapid proliferation of taverns was a concurrent phenomenon of coffee houses. In those times, as now, the coffee houses were viewed as more intellectually stimulating places (Starbucks had not yet been invented, you see) where the hatching and exchange of ideas would flow more freely.

But there was one problem: All that coffee was taking a toll at home. In a pamphlet called "The Women's Petition Against Coffee," printed in 1674 and circulated in London and across the pond as well, a now forgotten author railed against coffee, citing it as the cause of declining male performance. After a heavy session at the coffee house, the men returning home were "not able to stand to it, and in the very first Charge fall down flat." Your humble author assumes you know what is meant by "it."

Here in the colonies, Cock Ale played to several strengths: To say nothing of its supposed aphrodisiac qualities, it also illustrates early America's debt to home brewing, which itself produced a shadow economy to the tavern scene. Try our recipe and you'll agree: Nothing smells like home more than Cock Ale.

COCK ALE

To Make Cock Ale

Take five gallons of ale, and a large cock, the older the better. Parboil the cock, flay him, and stamp him in a stone mortar till his bones are broken (you must craw and gut him when you flay him), then put the cock into one quart of sack, and put to it one and one-half pounds of raisins of the sun stoned, some blades of mace, and a few cloves. Put all these into a canvas bag, and a little before you find the ale has done working, put the ale and bag together into a vessel. In a week or nine days' time bottle it up; fill the bottle but just above the neck, and give it the same time to ripen as other ale.

—From *Old-Time Recipes for Home Made Wines, Cordials and Liqueurs*
by Helen S. Wright, 1922

Cock Ale

OUR RECIPE

To capture our hypothesized idea of how the original Cock Ale may have tasted, our approach was to make a beer cocktail consisting of brown ale, sherry (sack), and a reduced chicken stock. Therefore, our recipe is of two parts: one for spicing chicken stock and another for the drink itself.

The Golden Chicken Stock recipe echoes all the flavors in the historic recipe we found: raisin, mace, and clove. Moreover, we discovered that this slightly spiced stock is excellent in any recipe calling for traditional chicken stock and is exceptional in Moroccan, Middle Eastern, and Indian recipes.

Considering that the original Cock Ale was used as a restorative health drink, our stock calls for ginger and turmeric, both praised for their anti-inflammatory properties and other health benefits. As well as a mild spice flavor, turmeric lends a rich golden-yellow color to the stock. The ratio of meat to bone in chicken wings gives the stock exceptional flavor and body.

NOTE: *We don't recommend using store-bought stock; it generally contains too much salt and does not have the flavor components (i.e., ginger, raisins, turmeric) that make our stock recipe work so well with the flavor of the Stock Ale (small beer). If you need to use store-bought stock, choose a low-sodium variety and infuse it with the flavors we call for in our recipe as it reduces.*

Golden Chicken Stock
MAKES ABOUT 1 GALLON (3.8 L)

4 pounds (1.8 kg) whole chicken wings
4 medium carrots, chopped into 1-inch
(2.5-cm) pieces (4 cups/450 g)
½ cup (75 g) golden raisins
1 (2-inch/5-cm) piece fresh ginger, peeled
and sliced

1 lemon, quartered
1 tablespoon whole black peppercorns
1 tablespoon salt
1½ teaspoons whole cloves
1 teaspoon ground turmeric
1 teaspoon ground mace

- Combine all the ingredients in a large stockpot and cover with water. Bring to a boil, then reduce the heat to low and simmer for 1½ hours, skimming off any foam that rises to the surface. Strain the stock through a cheesecloth-lined strainer and discard the solids. Chill the stock and remove any fat that solidifies on top.
- For the reduced stock for Cock Ale, boil 1 quart (960 ml) of the Golden Chicken Stock in a saucepan until reduced by half. Additional stock can be used for soups, stews, or curries. Refrigerate for up to 3 days or freeze for up to a month.

A short-cut using store-bought stock:

Pour 1 quart (960 ml) of low-sodium chicken stock into a medium saucepan with 2 tablespoons golden raisins, ½ teaspoon sliced peeled fresh ginger, ¼ teaspoon ground turmeric, ¼ teaspoon ground mace, ¼ teaspoon whole black peppercorns, 3 or 4 whole cloves, and a splash of fresh lemon juice. Reduce by half, strain, and use as called for in the Mock Cock Ale recipe.

Once you've got your stock, the rest is easy:

Mock Cock Ale
SERVES 1

¼ cup (60 ml) reduced Golden Chicken
Stock (above)
2 ounces (60 ml) dry sherry

1½ cups (360 ml) chilled brown ale or
Stock Ale (see recipe, page 21)

In a pint glass, combine the reduced chicken stock and dry sherry. Slowly top with the ale and serve.

DRINK UP!

In those early days, when those very first Americans had so little, what little they did have had to go a long way. And so ubiquitous beer wasn't merely about beer being the most easily accessible intoxicant, but also about its versatility. As these recipes (and Cock Ale, too) demonstrate, beer was food. As the Hot Flip shows us, beer was entertainment, too. Beer was a lot of things. But more than anything else, beer was good.

Some things never change.

TWO FLIPS

About two hundred years in the making—first spotted in the late 1600s, but morphing continuously until it was immortalized in the late 1800s in Jerry Thomas's *How to Mix Drinks or A Bon Vivant's Companion: The Bartender's Guide*—the flip is perhaps one of our oldest case studies in the evolution of the cocktail. In the loosest terms, flips began as beer with the addition of sugar and rum, heated into a froth by a red-hot poker. But over time, the cold flip developed as a less ostentatious answer, adding an egg and forgoing the theatrics of molten hot metal. Eventually, the cold flip would come to forsake beer altogether. But we present its more traditional varietal here, along with the original Hot Flip. (If you're looking for a truly early American flavor, swap in our Spruce Ale on page 26 for the Stock Ale.)

COLD FLIP
SERVES 1

2 ounces (60 ml) golden rum
½ ounce Ginger Syrup (see recipe, page 129)
1 raw egg

1 cup (240 ml) chilled brown ale or
    Stock Ale (see recipe, page 21)
Pinch of salt
Freshly grated nutmeg, for garnish

In a cocktail shaker, combine the rum, Ginger Syrup, egg, ale, and salt. Shake until all the ingredients are smooth and emulsified. Add ice to the shaker and shake again until the mixture is chilled. Strain into a tall glass and garnish with a couple gratings of nutmeg.

HOT FLIP
SERVES 1

2 ounces (60 ml) golden rum
1 tablespoon light molasses (see Note)
Pinch of salt
1 raw egg

1 cup (240 ml) chilled brown ale or
    Stock Ale (see recipe, page 21)
Freshly grated nutmeg

- In a pint glass, combine the rum, molasses, and salt; stir.

- Into another pint glass, crack the egg and beat well with a small whisk or fork.

- Pour the ale into a saucepan and add a couple gratings of nutmeg. Over medium heat, warm the ale until it begins to steam; do not boil. If the ale is too hot, it will curdle the egg.

- Add the warmed ale to the glass with the rum and molasses mixture. Pour in the beaten egg. Pour between the glasses until smooth and frothy, about 45 times.

- Transfer to a heatproof glass and garnish with a couple additional gratings of nutmeg.

NOTE: *Use light, baking, or dark molasses; avoid blackstrap, as the flavor is too bitter.*

RATTLE SKULL
SERVES 1

It is what it sounds like, my friend: a powerful admixture for only the most hearty drinker. We're talking about 3 to 4 ounces (90 to 120 ml) of hard liquor dropped into a pint of strong beer.

1¼ cups (300 ml) chilled brown ale or Stock Ale (see recipe, page 21)
1 ounce golden rum
1 ounce brandy
1 ounce fresh lime juice

½ ounce Brown Sugar Syrup (see recipe, page 124)
½ ounce Nutmeg Syrup (see recipe, page 129)
Pinch of cayenne pepper
Pinch of salt
Freshly grated nutmeg, for garnish

In a pint glass, combine all the ingredients but nutmeg and stir. Garnish with a couple gratings of nutmeg.

CALIBOGUS
SERVES 1

At the online project known as OEDILF—that's the Omnificent English Dictionary in Limerick Form, to you—one Kevin Lucas defines *calibogus* as the following:

If to taverns of yore you would come,
You could order spruce beer mixed with rum
And fermented molasses—
Maybe down several glasses
Of this drink calibogus. Ooh! Yum!

1 ounce golden rum
½ ounce light molasses
½ ounce fresh lime juice

1¼ cups (300 ml) Spruce Ale (see recipe, page 27)

In a cocktail shaker full of ice, combine the rum, molasses, and lime juice. Shake to combine and strain into a pint glass; top with the Spruce Ale.

COLONIAL SUNRISE
SERVES 1

Consider, for a moment, the American tomato: Spotted on this hallowed soil around 1710 in South Carolina, people were suspicious of it initially. First they thought it poisonous; then, responding to its sensual siren song, they used it as an ornament, but by the time Thomas Jefferson first ate one in Paris and sent seeds back home with instructions to grow them at the nearest opportunity, the American love affair with this most sumptuous of fruits had begun. It is in that spirit of discovery that we offer the Colonial Sunrise, the nightshade that brings the dawn (of the Bloody Mary).

Celery salt, for garnish
Lime wedge, for garnish
1¼ cups (300 ml) chilled brown ale or Stock
   Ale (see recipe, page 21)

3 ounces (90 ml) tomato juice
1 ounce fresh lime juice
1 teaspoon Worcestershire sauce, optional
23 dashes hot sauce, optional

- Onto a small plate or saucer, pour the celery salt in a thin layer. Wet the rim of a tall glass with a lime wedge and dip the glass into the celery salt, coating the edge. Set the glass aside.
- In a cocktail shaker, combine the ale, tomato juice, lime juice, and, if using, the Worcestershire and hot sauce. Stir to combine and pour into the celery salt–rimmed glass.

OL' SHANDY
SERVES 1

The history of the shandy—or shandygaff, if you're not into the whole brevity thing—is apocryphal at best. Gossip traces this mixture of beer and whatever soft drink is on hand to Henry VIII, who used it for his "marital difficulties"; this doesn't feel true, nor does another rendition, which puts its widespread adoption in the wake of Laurence Sterne's epic novel *The Life and Opinions of Tristram Shandy*. In either case, the shandy would have already been with us, as these are anecdotes, not origin stories. Perhaps the shandy was always here just waiting for you to notice it.

¾ cup (180 ml) chilled Ginger Beer
   (see recipe, page 137)

¾ cup (180 ml) chilled brown ale or Stock
   Ale (see recipe, page 21)
Lemon wedge, for garnish

Pour the ginger beer in a pint glass and top with the Stock Ale. Garnish with the lemon wedge.

COVENTRY CUP
SERVES 1

This dark, lovely, and tart drink—shandy-esque in its way, really—is something of a tribute to our fellow Northeasterners. For it's here where the raspberry grows, and often goes on for weeks at a time.

*1½ ounces Raspberry Shrub
(see recipe, page 131)
½ ounce fresh lime juice*

*1¼ cups (300 ml) chilled brown ale or
Stock Ale (see recipe, page 21)
Lime wedge, for garnish*

Combine the Raspberry Shrub and lime juice in a pint glass and top with the Stock Ale. Garnish with the lime wedge.

BISHOP'S WIFE
SERVES 1

There is a drink dating back to this era called the Bishop, which involves burning a bunch of oranges and pouring old wine over them, then dissolving a ton of sugar into the mix. This is not that drink. This is the Bishop's Wife, and she is much nicer.

*2 ounces (60 ml) golden rum
1 ounce Cherry Syrup (see recipe, page 130)
1 ounce Chocolate Syrup (see recipe,
page 130)*

*½ cup (120 ml) chilled brown ale or
Stock Ale (see recipe, page 21)
Fresh cherry, for garnish*

Fill a rocks glass with ice, add all the ingredients but the cherry, and stir to combine. Garnish with the cherry.

LAMBSWOOL
SERVES 4 TO 6

In his 1648 poem "Twelfth Night: Or, King and Queen," the lyric poet Robert Herrick does indeed stop off for a cup of Lambswool:

> *Next crown a bowl full*
> *With gentle lamb's wool:*
> *Add sugar, nutmeg, and ginger,*
> *With store of ale too;*
> *And thus ye must do*
> *To make the wassail a swinger.*

And he would know: Herrick, after all, most famously penned the line "gather ye rosebuds while ye may." And the Lambswool is in that #yolo spirit as well. Quite popular at Halloween, the drink is another one of those wassail-y drinks popular in eighteenth-century England. The name, of course, refers to the soft froth that the baked apples make when whisked with the warm ale, looking like nothing so much as lambswool.

4 apples, about 1½ pounds (680 g); choose a soft apple like McIntosh or Braeburn
4½ cups (1 L) brown ale or Stock Ale (see recipe, page 21)
3 cinnamon sticks
4 whole cloves
½ teaspoon freshly grated nutmeg
1 teaspoon grated peeled fresh ginger

- Preheat the oven to 350°F (175°C).
- Core the apples, place them in a roasting pan, and bake for about 40 minutes, or until very soft. Set aside until cool enough to handle but still warm.
- In a saucepan over medium-low heat, gently warm the ale. Add the cinnamon, cloves, nutmeg, and ginger.
- Cut the baked apples in half and scoop the flesh into a mixing bowl; discard the skins, cores, and seeds. With a fork, mash the apples until mostly smooth.
- Add the mashed apples to the saucepan with the spiced ale and whisk to combine.
- Keep this mixture at a bare simmer for 15 to 20 minutes to let the spices infuse.
- Right before serving, whisk vigorously to create a froth. Serve in heatproof glasses or mugs.

Ice Cream Ale
SERVES 4

First published in 1747, Hannah Glasse's *The Art of Cookery Made Plain and Easy* was a smash success and would have made Glasse the eighteenth-century equivalent to Martha Stewart—she even did time (albeit at the end of her life, in a debtor's prison). That business of unpleasantness aside, Glasse's contributions to gastronomy both in her native England and on these shores (where she was so popular that bootleg editions of her books were commonplace) cannot be underestimated. Many of them, for instance, are still made daily at the City Tavern here in Philadelphia.

Concurrent with Glasse's own life span was the invention, in fits and starts, of what we would now recognize as ice cream—or, to stay in period, "iced cream." And as you know, ice cream's popularity has *never* waned. Our Ice Cream Ale marries Glasse and the signature culinary invention of her time; Franklin, Washington, and Jefferson were all known to enjoy it as well, but they were hardly unique in this respect. After all, we all *scream* for it, do we not?

1 pint (473 ml) vanilla ice cream
1½ cups (360 ml) chilled brown ale or Stock
   Ale (see recipe, page 21)

1 ounce Vanilla Syrup (see recipe, page 129)
2 tablespoons malted milk powder
¼ teaspoon salt

In blender, combine all the ingredients. Blend until smooth and serve immediately.

Pumpkin Brown Ale
SERVES 1

Long before there were pumpkin spice lattes and pumpkin spice yogurt and pumpkin spice Nestle Toll House cookies and pumpkin spice kale chips and pumpkin spice sandwich bread, and their attendant backlash, there was, quite simply, the pumpkin. And the things were all over the place. In fact, their utter ubiquity during the eighteenth century made them a staple of early American brewing—not so much in the spirit of holiday pumpkin brews that line the shelves of bottle shops today, but as a more basic starter ingredient. Our recipe here allows for yesterday to meet today, where the earthy texture of actual pumpkin meets the sweetness associated with that flavor profile now.

1 tablespoon pumpkin puree
2 teaspoons Cinnamon Syrup (see recipe,
   page 129)

1 teaspoon Nutmeg Syrup (see recipe,
   page 129)
1½ cups (360 ml) chilled brown ale or
   Stock Ale (see recipe, page 21)

In a pint glass, combine the pumpkin puree and syrups and stir. Add about a third of the ale and stir to combine. Top with the remaining ale.

Chapter III

Cider

WHAT CIDER IS

If the early American settlers didn't already love cider with a devotion that rose to actual bodily need before they even arrived, the beverage would have likely shown up of its own accord. That is, if somebody didn't make it, it would have made itself. Left to its own devices in the wild, it nearly does: When you see an apple rotting in a grove, for instance, the very way it rots naturally suggests the beginnings of the cider-making process. The wild yeasts in the air around us, given the chance, will take to the apple like a moth to a flame, and vice versa. The apple *wants* to ferment; it is not a victim. Cider, too, is aspirational.

But before we get to that, let us look at the apple the way the colonials saw it: as a dietary essential, as a large piece of early America's agricultural, economic, and industrial puzzle and, not least, at long last, a victory, a sign that American *terroir* was not fallow.

The apple was among the very first things planted by the colonials—as early as 1623 at Plymouth—and it was one of the few early success stories.

"The apple is the most civilized of all trees. It is as harmless as a dove, as beautiful as a rose, and as valuable as flocks and herds. It has been longer cultivated than any other, and so is more humanized; and who knows but, like the dog, it will at length be no longer traceable to its wild original? It migrates with man, like the dog and horse and cow; first, perchance, from Greece to Italy, thence to England, thence to America; and our Western emigrant is still marching steadily toward the setting sun with the seeds of the apple in his pocket, or perhaps a few young trees strapped to his load."

—Henry David Thoreau, "Wild Apples," *The History of the Apple-Tree*

Unlike grains and vines, which consistently proved frustrating for farmers, the apple's spread was rapid and stretched quickly from New England to New Jersey, and then farther south.

It was a different apple than the ones we know today. What would have already been on the ground here in the 1600s when the first settlers arrived would have been either garland/sweet crab apples (*Malus coronaria*) or the southern crab apple variety (*Malus angustifolia*). These were native to the soil, and it's unclear if they were used by Native Americans.

In any case, contemporary palates—raised on flawless, tart Granny Smiths or Red Deliciouses—would have deemed them inedible, either impossibly

sour or garbage-y bland. And so, too, did the early settlers have their own feelings on the subject, importing seeds and grafts of other varieties from the Continent, which would eventually lead to America's first experiments with genetically modified (albeit farm-to-table) foods. (See page 54.)

The English palate (as well as the palates of others) would have already developed a taste for apples and cider, but in the colonies, where almost nothing was in abundance, the apple very much was, and quickly became, an essential part of the colonial diet. The apple tree gave us dried apples for winter; cider and applejack to drink; and cider vinegar as a medicine and preservative. The apple's ubiquity—and its ever-growing number of varieties—in fact came to symbolize agricultural longevity itself. More often than not, the planting of fruit trees was put down as a legal stipulation for land ownership; the very fact that a farmer had trees proved that he was planning on staying.

All this—to say nothing of its effervescent taste and natural powers of refreshment—would contribute to the everywhere-ness of cider. Its ascent was swift, thanks to the cheapness and abundance of the apple. And while the apple could be fashioned into a wide variety of alcoholic beverages—apple brandy, applejack, Calvados, and *eau de vie de cidre*—it was cider that reigned supreme. Even the otherwise teetotaling Puritans made an exception for it (often, in fact).

All along the East Coast, each farmer and distiller developed their own attendant lore establishing the uniqueness and superiority of their own apples and cider. New Jersey, for instance, claimed to be the greatest commercial outpost for cider; in New Hampshire, the Shakers made claims on the greatest qualities of cider. Franklin himself couldn't do without it, having care packages of the stuff sent to him when he was on long diplomatic sojourns overseas.

By the time American independence was won, one in ten New England farms also produced cider: It could be said that it was the stuff the nation was built on. Everybody drank it: John Adams, who quaffed a tankard of the beverage each and every morning, down to the average man on the street, who'd put away about thirty-five gallons per year.

Best of all, it was so available that it became a measure of availability itself—apples and cider, as well as their attendant seeds, pomaces, and grafts, became a most frequent item of barter. And like so many other things in these days, it was said to be good for you. Only in this case, that was probably right.

CIDER

What you have told us is all very good. It is indeed bad to eat Apples. It is better to make them all CIDER.

—Benjamin Franklin, in *Remarks Concerning the Savages of North America*, reporting an American Indian's response to hearing the story of Adam and Eve

CYDER FOR THE PRESENT USE

Procure a number of codlings, as juicy as you can get, but not too sweet, nor quite ripe; let them be laid in hay or straw that is very dry. When they have laid three days cut them into quarters and take out the hearts, then let them be bruised, and put into clean water, with a few blades of mace, and a handful of the tops of rosemary; mash all these together, and put to every twelve gallons two quarts of rhenish wine; when it has boiled two hours let it be drawn off, and set to cool, and it will be fit for use almost as soon as it is cold.

—From *The Farmer's Wife, Or, The Complete Country Housewife*, 1780

Hard Apple Cider

OUR RECIPE

MAKES 1 GALLON (3.8 L)

Supplies:

Small bowl
Whisk
2-gallon (7.5-L) fermenting bucket
Siphon

Bottle filler
12 (12-ounce/360-ml) bottles
Bottle caps and capper

Ingredients:

1 gallon (3.8 L) pasteurized apple cider
1 packet (0.2 ounces/5 g) champagne yeast

½ cup (120 ml) water, at 95°F (35°C)

Sanitize all equipment prior to beginning.

- Pour the apple cider into a 2-gallon (7.5-L) fermenting bucket.

- In a small bowl, whisk together the yeast and water to combine. Let stand until the mixture begins to bubble, about 10 minutes.

- Add the yeast mixture to the apple cider in the fermenting bucket and stir to combine. Place the lid on the bucket and seal with a stopper and air lock. Store at room temperature for 10 to 14 days.

- After 10 to 14 days of fermentation, rack the cider into a sanitized 1-gallon (3.8-L) glass container. Seal the container with a stopper and air lock. Store at room temperature and away from direct sunlight for 4 weeks.

- After 4 weeks, the cider will be ready to drink—or it can be bottled and stored.

VINEGAR: CIDER'S OTHER GIFT

BUT WAIT, cider seems to want to say, always, THERE'S MORE! Cider didn't simply drive a two-century-long apple boom in America on its own steam; it also carved out a niche as both a culinary necessity and catchall home remedy—with essentially what amounted to its old, leftover self. You see, when left out, cider will eventually oxidize its own ethyl alcohol element, which will then convert into acetaldehyde and then, later, into acetic acid. All of which is a fancy way of saying that cider also gives us apple cider vinegar—or, as it is known to your local health food store stockist or homeopath, ACV.

Cider has fallen in and out of fashion over the years since the 1700s, but as it happened, ACV became cider's lasting gift to both American cuisine and medicine. In those colonial days—centuries before refrigeration—vinegar touched nearly everything. On one hand, it was necessary to pickle vegetables if one wanted them to keep over the long winter months; on the other, ACV also lent itself to use as a working home remedy to any number of maladies, from dandruff to stomach problems. And it's still in use under both of those tents today.

But it's pickling with vinegar that still informs the modern American palate. No wonder: Our ancestors did a lot of it. Wine vinegar was available as an import then, but like so many other products in common use across the Atlantic, it was prohibitively expensive. Eventually, cider vinegar became so widely used that it was a significant domestic product, fetching a price 300 percent greater than its plain cider ancestor. And, of course, it's trendy once again today.

✕✕ ✕ ✕✕ ✕ ✕ ✕ ✕✕ ✕ ✕✕ ✕ ✕ ✕ ✕ ✕✕ ✕ ✕

CIDER VINEGAR

The poorest sort of cider will serve for vinegar, in managing which proceed thus: First draw off the cider into a cask that has had vinegar in it before; then put some of the apples that have been pressed into it, set the whole in the sun, and in a week or nine days it may be drawn off into another cask. This is a good table vinegar.

—From *Five Thousand Receipts in All the Useful and Domestic Arts* by Colin MacKenzie, 1825

Apple Cider Vinegar

OUR RECIPE

This a great way to use the leftover apple scraps from baking a pie or tart. Since we are using the apple peels, it is preferred to use organic and unwaxed fruit. If the apples are waxed, scrub them well under warm water until the wax is removed.

CIDER VINEGAR #1
MAKES ABOUT 1 QUART (960 ML)

Peels and cores of 6 to 8 apples, about
4 pounds (1.8 kg)

¼ cup (60 ml) honey
Filtered water

- Place the apples in a clean 1-quart (960-ml) glass jar. Dissolve the honey in the water and pour the mixture over the apples.
- Be sure all the apples are submerged. A smaller jar lid can be used to weigh down the apple scraps if necessary.
- Cover the mouth of the jar with a coffee filter or a double layer of cheesecloth and secure with a rubber band.
- Store the jar in a dark, warm place for 10 days. The liquid should begin to gently bubble.
- After 10 days, strain the liquid, discarding the apple scraps. Return the liquid to the jar, cover it again with a coffee filter or cheesecloth, secure with a rubber band, and store.
- Taste the vinegar every week until it is strong enough. Seal the jar and store in the refrigerator for up to 6 months.

Cider Vinegar #2

1 quart (960 ml) hard apple cider

- Pour the cider into a clean 1-quart (960-ml) glass jar, leaving about 2 inches (5 cm) of headspace.
- Cover the mouth of the jar with a coffee filter or a double layer of cheesecloth and secure with a rubber band.
- Store the jar in a dark, warm place for 2 to 4 weeks.
- During that time, the mother will form. Once the vinegar has reached the desired strength, strain out the mother and set it aside to make more vinegar. Bottle and store the vinegar in the refrigerator indefinitely.

NOTE: *Vinegar may appear cloudy, or a gray mass may form on the top. This is known as the mother and it can be used to quickly create new batches of vinegar.*

JOHNNY APPLESEED &
THE SWEDENBORGIAN MYSTICS

What so lurks in the American imagination about Johnny Appleseed that we seem to want to wish him into fiction? Is it the way we're taught about him as children, that there was once a sweet but robust young man who traveled the countryside preaching self-reliance and good health by way of the American apple? Or was it the myth that he constructed for himself that we're still responding to hundreds of years later?

No matter what the answers, if indeed they could ever be definitively known, there are some simple facts at hand: John Chapman, aka Johnny Appleseed, was born September 26, 1774, in Leominster, Massachusetts. A deeply religious man, possessed also of an abiding love for animals, nature, and a nomadic lifestyle, Appleseed really did head from Pennsylvania out into Ohio, Indiana, and Illinois, what was then the Western frontier, planting apple trees. (The "seed" part is myth of a sort; what he really did was

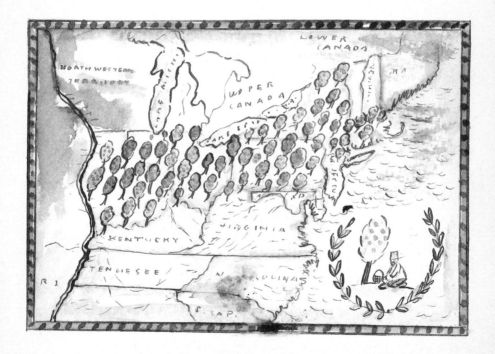

plant orchards as a sort of franchise operation, returning every year or two to check on them.) And all along the way, he evangelized not just for apples but for what amounted to, for him, a spiritual view that was of the utmost importance—a kind of cobbled-together American mysticism that claimed direct contact with God, angels, and spirits.

And somewhere in there, he just might have been the first American of a type we not only recognize but are fully overtaken by today. Although Johnny Appleseed wasn't born until just before American independence, in so many ways, the man and his legend are the sum total of what had been brewing in the American imagination for more than 150 years. Whereas so many of our noted American forefathers were still deeply English in both the way they carried themselves and their deeply principled—to the point of being buttoned-down—natures, in Johnny Appleseed we have perhaps the first American archetype bearing traits recognizable in ourselves today. We are impatient—we want what we want and we want it now—while at the same time priding ourselves on being neighborly, some of us even claiming that we are instruments of God's will.

As he went from town to town on his unique agri-missionary tour, Appleseed spun his own self-invention into American myth, beginning a tradition of a type of man that runs through our history—and Jefferson, Adams, and Franklin be damned, had more influence on the types of people we'd be than they did. Ben Franklin doesn't lead to a Joseph Smith or a Jimmy Swaggart or Scientology, but Johnny Appleseed almost exclusively does.

What drove him? Same thing as the other guys: God stuff.

Appleseed was a high-ranking member of the New Church, or a Swedenborgian—that is, a follower of Emanuel Swedenborg, the eighteenth-century scientist-turned-theologian who would eventually claim himself as a messenger of God's own word.

Briefly, here is Swedenborg: The son of a heretic father believes in communion with God and angels and spirits in everyday life; he begins his life and career in reason and science. And he's quite accomplished, too: He makes early sketches for a flying machine. He is credited with first conceptualizing the neuron, and is quite prescient about many other discoveries that would come into view in the century ahead. Nevertheless, something is missing. He suffers from a stutter. And in 1718, Swedenborg publishes an article that attempts to explain spiritual and mental events in terms of minute vibrations, or "tremulations." From here on, he is on a path that will take him through the rest of his life: The more he learns and discovers, the more he is drawn to metaphysical matters.

He begins to keep a dream journal, the contents of which are both sublime and horrific, which some believe to be a secret narrative of his own will battling God's. He begins to have visions. The visions tell him that he is the Lord, and to act accordingly and write the word of God. He has gone nuts.

He embarks upon writing a tome called *Arcana Caelestia*, a magnum opus parsing the spiritual meaning of every verse in the Bible. He also believes that judgment day has already come and gone, and that he'd seen the whole thing; no one else noticed because the revelation was made known to him only. As John "Johnny Appleseed" Chapman approaches adulthood, a Swedenborgian church of North America—it called the New Church and exists to this day—is popular, and he becomes one of its leading evangelists.

Now, I know what you are thinking: *Et tu, Johnny Appleseed?* And that is certainly one very reasonable way of looking at it. On the other hand, put the man in his times, times of searching that aspired for certain men to be godlike in all things, godlike in their freedoms and their courage to make their ambitions real. These were men who looked out on the American horizon and saw in its fields and in its own brand of moonlight something beckoning them to a destiny the world had never known before and would never know again. So, while you don't get L. Ron Hubbard without Johnny, you don't get Walt Whitman, either.

You also don't get nearly as much sweet, effervescent cider, a salve for whatsoever ails your poor human body and soul.

A Brief List of Apple Varieties in Great Abundance During the Colonial Era

When colonials first began to plant apple trees on this hallowed soil, they found that here, as in the old countries, class separated them in what they had to work with. Poor farmers generally started their orchards with seeds and pomace (remains from previous harvests); the wealthier would have had access to custom-made grafts, which would produce seedlings of potentially infinite varieties. But in a stunning metaphor for the sociology of the coming independent and free America itself, it is also the case that apple seeds won't produce the same variety as their original tree. What resulted then was a wild variety of apples that, when you take it in as the list here, is but a small reminder of the richness of the old world. In 1905, there were fourteen thousand apple varieties available in these United States; today, there are less than a hundred, with but a paltry fifteen listed on the U.S. Apple Association's website. What follows are apples that, by and large, we'll never know again. But we can dream of them.

A

American Pippin
American Nonpariel
Autumn or Fall
  Pippin
Aunt's Apple

B

Baldwin or Pecker
  Apple
Baltimore Apple
Black Apple
Brownite
Bow Apple
Bell Flower
Bullock's Pippin or
  Sheep's Snout

C

Campfield or Newark
  Sweeting
Cathead
Catline
Carthouse or Gilpin
Cider Apple or
  Codling
Corlies Sweet
Cooper's Russeting

F

Flat Sweeting or
  Hornet Sweeting

G

Gloucester White
Golden Pippin
Golden Rennet
Green Everlasting
Green Newton
  Pippin
Grey House

H

Hagloe Crab
Harrison Apple or
  Long Stem
Harly Sweeting
High-Top Sweeting
Holmes Apple
Holten Sweeting
Hughes's Virgina
  Crab

L

Lady Apple
Lady Finger
Large Red and Green
  Sweeting
Large Early Harvest
Loring Sweeting
Large Yellow
  Newark Pippin/
  Yellow Pippin/
  French Pippin of
  Newark

M

Maiden's Blush
Michael Henry
Monstrous Pippin or
  American Gloria
  Mundi
Morgan Apple

N

Newark King Apple
Nonsuch
Nursery Apple

P

Pearmain
Pennock's Red Winter
Priestly
Pove-shon
Pound Apple

Q

Quince Apple
Queen Apple

R

Rariton Sweeting
Red Everlasting
Redling
Red Streak
Rambo
Roane's White Crab
Rhode Island
  Greening
Roman Stem

Royal Pearmain

Royal Pearmain
Royal Russet or
  Leather Coat
Roxbury Russeting
Ruckman's Pearmain
  or Golden
  Pearmain

S

Seek No Further
Spitszenburgh
Spice Apple
Styre
Summer Pearmain
Swaar Apple
Sweet Greening

T

Tolman Sweeting

V

Vandevere
Vanwinkle or
  Granniwinkle

W

Wine Apple
Wine Sap

Y

Yellow Sweeting
Gilliflower Apple
Sweeney Nonpariel
  Apple

—Culled from *The American Orchardist: Or, A Practical Treatise on the Culture and
Management of Apple and Other Fruit Trees, with Observations on the Diseases to which
They are Liable, and Their Remedies. To which Is Added the Most Approved Method of Manufacturing
and Preserving Cider, and Also Wine from Apple Juice and Currants.* Adapted to the Use of
American Farmers, and All Lovers and Cultivators of Fine Fruit by James Thacher, 1825

"O Bid the Cider Flow"

The associations with early American life and cider run so deep that, to the folklorist, they provide as vibrant a connection between the Old World and the New World as there is. And given the beverage's qualities—cider is sparkling; cider is friendly; cider is for everyone—it should come as no surprise that cider was well represented in folksong on both sides of the Atlantic. "O Bid the Cider Flow" was but one song—originating in Devon and Cornwall but circulating across the pond, no doubt—of a catalog of cider-related tunes. (For more, check out the online archives of Smithsonian Folkways at http://siarchives.si.edu/collections.)

THE APPLE TREE

As the season doth advance,
    Your apples for to gather,
I bid you catch the chance
    To pick them in fine weather.
    O the jovial days, &c.

When to a pummy ground,
    You squeeze out all the juice, sir,
Then fill a cask well bound,
    And set it by for use, sir.
O bid the cider flow
    In ploughing and in sowing,
The healthiest drink I know
    In reaping and in mowing.
    O the jovial days, &c.

—Culled from *A Book of the West: Being an Introduction to Devon and Cornwall, Volume 2*, by Sabine Baring-Gould, Methuen & Co., 1899

Ciderkin,
You Know, for Kids!

Cider was such an important part of the diet in colonial days that a word emerged for the beverage derived from cider often given to small children—ciderkin. More a word than an actual recipe—it is literally dregs of adult cider makings with water poured in and then mixed with molasses or ginger—ciderkin is notable because it's a rarity in that a separate beverage was made for children at all in those times. As often as not, kids drank the hard stuff, too.

APPLEJACK,
OR JERSEY LIGHTNING

In the logbooks of American vice, there is a long tradition of rough-hewn, homemade substances that are more or less designed (or appropriated) to drive their takers out of their ever-loving minds. Today, there are meth, and bath salts, and molly, and all their affiliated subvariants. One hundred years or so ago, during Prohibition, there was rotgut and moonshine and bathtub gin. But before that, there was applejack, a perversion of our beloved cider so strong that one cannot help but be fascinated by it. There is hard cider, of course, but applejack is another beast entirely. And while there are beverages claiming to be applejack available commercially today, they are applejacks in name only. The difference? A process that produces a beverage of alcoholic potency that borders on out-and-out toxicity.

Whereas most distilled beverages come about through heat, applejack's raw process is the result of the coldest temperatures possible. Roughly put, applejack is cider left out to freeze for months at a time; during that time, the part of the cider that is water freezes, and that which is alcohol separates itself. Over days and weeks, this process repeats, night after night and day after day, until what is left over is the hard, hard, very hard stuff—a concentrated alcohol strong in proof, loaded with strange impurities, and intoxicating to the point of bodily danger. If it sounds awesome, that's because it is. Sadly, this is as much as we are legally allowed to say about applejack. Instead, please stay alive and enjoy these other perfectly safe and delicious cider-adjacent recipes.

PERRY

Procure a number of ripe pears proportioned to the liquor you intend to make, and mix them with a few crabs; then let the whole be properly mashed together, until the liquor appears, which must be strained through a cloth, or a very fine sieve, then put to it a little yeast, and when it has worked three days, let it be drawn into another vessel, in which it must stand ten days, when it will be ready to be bottled off, and you may drink it as soon as you please.

—From *The Farmer's Wife, Or, The Complete Country Housewife*, 1780

Make this according to directions for apple cider. Among the caricatures of the day (just after Perry's victory on Lake Erie, 1813) was one representing John Bull, in the person of the King, seated, with his hand pressed upon his stomach, indicating pain, which the fresh juice of the pear, called perry, will produce. This caricature is entitled "Queen Charlotte and Johnny Bull got their dose of Perry."

—From *Old-Time Recipes for Home Made Wines, Cordials and Liqueurs*
by Helen S. Wright, 1922

Perry

OUR RECIPE

MAKES 1 GALLON (3.8 L)

1 gallon (3.8 L) pasteurized pear juice
½ cup (120 ml) water, at 95°F (35°C)

1 packet (0.2 ounces/5 g) champagne yeast

Sanitize all equipment prior to beginning.

- Pour the pear juice into a 2-gallon (7.5-L) fermenting bucket.
- In a small bowl, whisk together the water and yeast to combine. Let stand until the mixture begins to bubble, about 10 minutes.
- Add the yeast mixture to the pear juice in the fermenting bucket and stir to combine. Place the lid on the bucket and seal with a stopper and air lock. Store at room temperature for 10 to 14 days.
- After 10 to 14 days, rack the perry into a sanitized 1-gallon (3.8-L) glass container. Seal the container with a stopper and air lock. Store the container at room temperature and away from direct sunlight for 4 weeks. After 4 weeks of fermentation, the perry will be ready to drink—or it can be bottled and stored.

TERROIRISM

Cider would not wane in popularity until the country's very makeup began to shift in the mid-1800s; by then, Germans and northern Europeans would arrive in droves, asserting the primacy of beer that persists to this day. Even so, the comeback cider enjoys today is not even a shadow of its former self. But if the trend supersedes anything other than that, and cider once again weaves its way back into its rightful place in our hearts, it would have the potential to right many wrongs we've made along the way—not least among them, the idea that American indigenous soil, or *terroir*, is something that we should be recultivating.

During the heyday of American cider, so many varieties were offered that a connoisseurship developed. An advanced cider palate, not unlike that of an oenophile, would be able to detect the cider's *terroir*—the apple's regional characteristics and complexities. Agricultural societies and local organizations in apple-rich communities—and there were many—would encourage such distinctions. After all, the distinguished palate would have to be that of one who consumed a lot of cider. These communities saw more notable cider varietals as a source of local pride, much like our European cousins take pride in their wine.

But ultimately, cider wasn't wine—to its great credit.

DRINK UP!

Of all of the recipes in this book, these cider treasures may feel the most alive. As the microbrew revolution has given way to an expanded interest in cider, each cider recipe that follows wouldn't be out of place in your local gastropub. Luckily, they will outlive the word "gastropub," too.

MULLED CIDER

SERVES 4 TO 6

Our man in the kitchen refers to this as "colonial autumn in a cup," which we can only take to mean that it's so good you'd go without antibiotics, kill a Brit with a musket, and freeze your ass off just to enjoy a cup with your friends. Luckily, you don't have to do that (again) (yet). And so here it is, the classic: heavy on apple pie spices such as cinnamon, nutmeg, ginger, and clove, in a portion appropriate for serving you plus three to five fellow agitators.

3 cups (720 ml) Hard Apple Cider
  (see recipe, page 47)
4 cinnamon sticks
9 whole cloves
3 star anise pods

½ teaspoon freshly grated nutmeg
1 tablespoon grated peeled fresh ginger
1 orange, thinly sliced
½ cup (120 ml) brandy
Honey, optional

In a large saucepan, combine the cider, spices, and orange slices. Over medium heat, bring the mixture just to a simmer (boiling too hard will evaporate all the alcohol). Slightly cover the saucepan and continue to simmer for 10 to 15 minutes. Remove from the heat. Ladle the cider into heatproof glasses, top each with a nip of brandy and a spoonful of honey (if desired) and serve.

SNAKEBITE
SERVES 1

The Snakebite is a modern monstrosity that calls to mind nothing so much as the indelibly awful Alannah Myles's international Top 10 hit from 1989, "Black Velvet," which is also a thing that some people call the Snakebite. Bill Clinton was famously refused one in England, proving that while we may have won our independence, the Brits got to keep their dignity. Even so, we can admit (though not in mixed company, of course) . . . it's not bad.

1 cup (240 ml) Hard Apple Cider   *1 cup (240 ml) brown ale or Stock Ale*
   (see recipe, page 47)   *(see recipe, page 21)*

Pour the cider into a pint glass. Slowly top with the ale.

SNAKEBITE AND BLACK
SERVES 1

1 cup (240 ml) Hard Apple Cider   *1 tablespoon Blackberry Shrub*
   (see recipe, page 47)   *(see recipe, page 131)*
1 cup (240 ml) brown ale or Stock Ale
   (see recipe, page 21)

Pour the cider into a pint glass. Slowly top with the ale and Blackberry Shrub.

STONE FENCE
SERVES 1

There comes a time in everyone's life when you've got to do something brave or awful, and you know like you know your own face that the only way to get through it is to get smashed beforehand. And so it goes with the deeply boozy Stone Fence, the preferred drink of Colonel Ethan Allen's ever-loyal Green Mountain Boys militia, who quaffed the stuff in advance of many bouts of grievous, ponderous violence.

2 ounces (60 ml) dark rum   *1¼ cups (300 ml) Hard Apple Cider*
                               (see recipe, page 47)

Pour the rum into a pint glass full of ice. Top with the hard cider.

DEVIL'S BANG
SERVES 1

Whiskey and cider in the same glass: The Devil made us do it.

2 ounces (60 ml) Spiced Whiskey
  (see recipe, page 187)

1¼ cups (300 ml) chilled Hard Apple Cider
  (see recipe, page 47)

Pour the spiced whiskey into a pint glass full of ice. Top with the hard cider.

CHERRY JACK
SERVES 1

Sayeth the man behind the bar: "This one's inspired by the traditional Jack Rose cocktail: Instead of grenadine, which is made from pomegranates, we are using cherry syrup and bitters. Cherries remind me of George Washington. I cannot tell a lie."

  It's true. He can't. He's got syrup all over his face.

2 ounces (60 ml) applejack
½ ounce Cherry Syrup (see recipe, page 129)
½ ounce fresh lemon juice

12 dashes of Cherry Bitters (see recipe,
  page 166)
Lemon twist, for garnish

- In a cocktail shaker full of ice, combine the applejack, Cherry Syrup, lemon juice, and Cherry Bitters.

- Shake until chilled, strain into a martini glass, and garnish with the lemon twist.

ORCHARD MIMOSA

SERVES 1

The hangover begat the flip; the flip, in time, gave itself over to the Bucks Fizz; and shortly thereafter, the mimosa was the answer to the Fizz. Eventually, they put bacon and eggs next to it, and called it the $50 brunch. The historian, the sentimentalist, the curmudgeon all want to ask, *But wasn't something lost along the way?* Well, not really. But if you want to drink the *Bill & Ted's Excellent Adventure* version of this book, here it is: the little morning pick-me-up Ben Franklin would have had, if Ben was a Samantha.

3 ounces (90 ml) chilled fresh orange juice
3 ounces (90 ml) chilled Hard Apple Cider
  (see recipe, page 47)

Dash of Orange Bitters (see recipe,
  page 165)
Orange wedge, for garnish

Add the orange juice to a champagne flute. Top with the cider and bitters. Garnish with the orange wedge.

CIDER BEE

SERVES 1

Since antiquity, people have been looking to Apple Cider Vinegar as a cure for any number of maladies, from indigestion to yeast infections to cancer. Here is the crazy part: There's something to all of this. ACV won't ward off death (what does?), but it seems to exist chemically in a magic zone of overlap that rings all kinds of healthy bells.

To celebrate its existence, we suggest you mix it with gin, honey, and soda water. If that's not enough for you to celebrate, think of it as an experiment: However you are feeling now, you will probably feel better. Science!

1 tablespoon Apple Cider Vinegar (see
  recipe, page 49)
1 tablespoon honey

1½ ounces gin or Garden Gin
  (see recipe, page 167)
½ cup (120 ml) soda water
Lemon wedge, for garnish

In cocktail shaker full of ice, combine the vinegar, honey, and gin. Shake to combine. Strain into a rocks glass full of ice and top with the soda water. Garnish with the lemon wedge.

CIDER SANGRIA
SERVES 6

Sangria predates Christ, when Romans first decided to mix wine with water in an effort to sidestep the effects of dirty water. And it was the dirty water of England, of course, that made the colonists suspicious of clean North American water, which actually would have been fine for them to drink, right up until the moment when they'd made that clean water absolutely filthy, just like the water they had at home, but by which point they'd been subsisting on beers, ales, and ciders anyway. Do you see? Do you see that history is so often the story of man making the same stupid mistake over and over again? We raise this glass of Cider Sangria in flustered tribute to all mankind, including ourselves. Truly, it's a miracle we're able to even dress ourselves each morning.

2 cups (480 ml) Hard Apple Cider
   (see recipe, page 47)
½ cup (120 ml) applejack or apple brandy
½ cup (120 ml) apple juice

1½ ounces fresh lemon juice
1 apple, unpeeled, quartered and thinly
   sliced

Add all the ingredients to a pitcher and stir to combine. Refrigerate until chilled, about 1 hour. Serve in glasses full of ice garnished with some of the soaked apple slices.

CIDER SHANDY
SERVES 1

By and large, most homes during the colonial era did not feature patios on which to enjoy shandies. Pity.

¾ cup (180 ml) chilled Hard Apple Cider
   (see recipe, page 47)

¾ cup (180 ml) chilled Ginger Ale
   (see recipe, page 137)
Lemon wedge, for garnish

Add the cider to a pint glass and top with the ginger ale. Garnish with the lemon wedge.

CHAPTER IV

WINE

THE AMERICAN WINE EXPERIMENT

For all of America's wildly successful experiments that have won us favor throughout mankind—democracy, the abolition of a class system, jazz, denim, Bill Murray, to name but a few—we have, all the same, been dogged by a handful of persistent failures. The optimist will say, "Well, no one can do it all." The pragmatist will say, "Well, why would you want to?" And the pessimist will say, "Get this disgusting wine away from me."

Because it's the production of wine that has historically been among America's greatest failures—second only to our race relations in terms of things that, since day one, we simply cannot get right. And while we still hold out hope for the equality of all men and women (it's in our charter, after all), we hold no such hope for making high-quality wine (thankfully, we're not on the hook for that).

We could in the United States make as great a variety of wines as are made in Europe; not exactly of all the same kinds, but doubtlefs as good.

—Thomas Jefferson, writing in his journal in 1808, and who has still not been proven right

But still, since the 1600s, we have tried. And I know what you're thinking: What about California? What about the Willamette Valley? Noble efforts, yes; some of them are even drinkable. But are they Frankenvines, the results of technology and the hubris of wealthy dilettantes? That is for you to judge. Even in the case of your approval and the offense I can now clearly see on your face, even you, Mr. Coppola, must concede that the production of drinkable American wine is a recent development in our history.

The timeline is dotted with the type of failures normally associated with long-suffering baseball teams. Colonists first attempted to make wine in the late 1500s in what is now Jacksonville, Florida. It was as ridiculous an idea then as it is now. A more concerted effort to start American vineyards was

attempted in 1619 with imported French *vinifera* vines; they were met with pestilence and vine disease. Rinse and repeat, over and over again. Throughout, a set of prejudices and questions emerged: Can American *terroir* produce a good wine? And if it can't, what does this say about us? In America, is wine only for the wealthy who can afford to pay for that which is brought from overseas?

They're questions that are still being asked.

Eventually—and by eventually I mean by the 1800s—grapes were successfully grown, and a beverage mutually agreed upon to be wine was fashioned. But from our earliest colonial days, wine has been a difficult proposition. Even one of our bibles about the world of colonial drinking—*Early American Beverages* by John Hull Brown—gracefully demurs in its chapter on the subject. Its preamble talks about wine in ancient Greece where it might address the same in ancient Virginia; its lead-off recipes pull from British archives; and its American recipes for wine are basically wine-ish ciders. Brown could hardly be blamed. As we say: No one can do it all.

Aw, hell, let's try one more time anyway.

QUINCE WINE

Clean your quinces thoroughly, then grate them, and press through a linen cloth. To every pound of liquor put two pounds of double-refined sugar. When the sugar is dissolved pour off the liquor into another vessel, in which it must stand a week without being stopped, for the more air gets into the better. Then stop up the cask, and when it has stood six months bottle it off; and it will be fit for use when it has been bottled a week.

—From *The Farmer's Wife, Or, The Complete Country Housewife*, 1780

Quince Wine

OUR RECIPE

MAKES 1 GALLON (3.8 L)

21 quinces
4 cups (800 g) sugar
Zest and juice of 3 lemons
1 Campden tablet

1 cup (240 ml) fresh orange juice,
    at room temperature
1 package (0.2 ounces/5g) wine yeast
1 teaspoon yeast nutrient

Sanitize all equipment prior to beginning.

- Grate the quinces, getting as close to the cores as possible, and put the grated fruit in a large stockpot. Add just enough water to cover the quince and bring to a boil. Reduce the heat to medium and to cook for 15 minutes.

- After cooking, strain the quince mixture through a cheesecloth-lined strainer into a sanitized 2-gallon (7.5-L) fermenting bucket. Press on the solids with the back of a wooden spoon to extract as much liquid as possible. Discard the solids.

- Add the sugar and lemon zest and juice and allow the mixture to cool to room temperature. Add the Campden tablet, cover, and let sit for 24 hours.

- Pour the orange juice into a clean 1-pint (480-ml) jar. Add the wine yeast and yeast nutrient, stir to combine, and cover. Let sit for 1 to 2 hours, until the yeast is activated and bubbling.

- Add the orange juice–yeast mixture to the fermenting bucket with the quince mixture. If necessary, add enough water to make 1 gallon (3.8 L) of liquid. Cover and seal the fermenting bucket with an air lock and ferment for 2 to 3 days.

- Pour the liquid into a sanitized 1-gallon (3.8-L) glass jug and seal with an air lock. Let the wine ferment for 6 to 9 months before bottling and drinking.

THOMAS JEFFERSON, ARISTOCRATIC DRINKER

Thomas Jefferson is, without a doubt, early America's most notable oenophile. And to look at him in that aspect alone only serves to highlight just how much there was to the man, who is perhaps the Colonial era's most interesting figure. A statesman with an artistic temperament who stretched the very boundaries of the term *Renaissance man*, he may not ever be fully understood within the average person's cursory grasp of history. There is simply almost too much to him.

As a wine enthusiast alone, though, he is notable. As a young man, when he first came to the colonies, Jefferson would have enjoyed the imported wine then favored by gentlemen who could afford it, Madeira. This fortified wine from Portugal was heavy, syrupy stuff, not easily drinkable, but nevertheless indicated status. (Madeira's rise in the colonies was itself a product of shipping convenience as much as it was prevailing tastes of the times.)

But as Jefferson's palate developed, so too did his interest in wine, to the point of obsession. He kept an impressive cellar throughout his life, traveling extensively in France and Italy as a combination wine tourist/diplomat, and he kept detailed notes. Before long, Jefferson also kept a cellar in Paris, and he essentially tithed his income to the grape. By the time he held the presidency, his interest had ballooned to the point where, during his years in office, he acquired up to twenty thousand bottles of wine. Eventually, he came to favor Bordeaux and Burgundy. (See "Jefferson's Reds," page 74.)

Once out of office, he tried for no less than two decades to establish vineyards at his Monticello home, using the finest vines and expertise money could buy. But it was no use: His efforts there met the same fates of pests, ill weather, and bad luck that had plagued so many other ambitious would-be vintners. He never produced a single bottle of wine.

He excelled at cider, though.

Jefferson's Reds

Thanks in large part to the impressive cellar he kept—it would have been notable even if he did not have a standing date with history—as well as his own meticulous notes, there is a formidable body of scholarship on Thomas Jefferson and his specific relationship with wine—a relationship that was, as is the case with any great student, always on the move. "For the present," he wrote in his notes in 1816, "I confine myself to the physical want of some good Montepulciano . . . , this being a very favorite wine, and habit having rendered the light and high flavored wines a necessary of life with me." The third president of the United States kept impeccable records of wines he'd tasted and acquired, and curiously, his preferences would not be out of place on a well-kept wine list today. Here, for instance, is a brief selection of reds from his wine list, appellations that are still in circulation:

Red Bordeaux
Château Haut-Brion
Lafite
Latour
Margaux

Rhone Valley
Côte-Rôtie

Red Burgundies
Chambertin
Clos de Vougeot
Vosne-Romanée
Volna

MADEIRA

In lieu of any worthy domestic product, one imported varietal of wine emerged as early America's clear favorite: Madeira. This fortified Portuguese wine from the port of the same name has its origin story in the first explorations to the New World during the 1400s. Some three and a half centuries later, it would also become synonymous with American independence. But before we get to that, we need to explore what it is. Because like America, Madeira is a kind of happy accident.

In the course of shipping their wines across the seas, Portuguese vintners discovered something when fortifying their wines to stand up to long periods of travel—once they did, Madeira became very much its own thing. The process, briefly, goes something like this: Vintners take traditionally made wines of the Madeira region and add in neutral grape spirits—think a sort of modified vodka or eau de vie—to fortify it. From there, the wine is "cooked" to 140°F (60°C) for an extended period and oxidized. (The cooking and oxidizing process would have been more subtle and not even carried out by human hands back in the 1700s, however; rather, long journeys in sweltering conditions would have completed this part naturally.)

The idea—and what made Madeira so durable and, in turn, beloved by early Americans—is that the wine is essentially spoiled, professionally and on purpose. Thus, it never really "goes bad." And I mean never: At the time of this writing, one could—if one wished to and had, say, a spare few grand lying around—sample a bottle of Madeira from 1790. They're still around.

Even better, the process enabled vintners to craft both dry and sweet varieties of Madeira, thereby making it applicable across a range of situations.

Essentially crafted for long journeys by sea, what was really behind any Madeira preference at all is that the wine was exempted from taxation—due to an exclusive trade deal between Britain and Portugal. Nearly every other imported wine was subject to sizable duties. Even so, Madeira wasn't cheap. Common people wouldn't have drunk it—or, at least, not often—but that didn't stop it from becoming part and parcel of the story of the American Revolution. During the American Revolutionary War, Madeira became the leading import as well as a totem of nascent patriotism in the same way that coffee did. Only we liked Madeira more.

Jefferson toasts the Declaration of Independence with it. He starts his career as an oenophile with it, and ends it that way, too. But it's first politicized when John Hancock arrives in port at Boston in 1768 and British agents attempt to levy duties on his haul of 3,150 gallons of the stuff. He refuses; British authorities seize Hancock's boat and its contents, and Boston riots. From that point on, Madeira is identified with the American struggle for independence, so much so that an informal consensus arises among colonials of the era: Madeira belongs to them.

"You are a wonder of nature and for all people a certain cure," or:

The Antimonial Cup

Frustrating as it may have been for the ever-cursed winemaker, the wine that colonists were able to produce was at least good for one thing: With the aid of something called the antimonial cup, it would never fail to induce vomiting.

A staple of premodern medicine, the antimonial cup served as a "physick" tool used to clear out those who needed clearing out. The cup itself, as you can see, looked not unlike a neti pot, but was made of glass and treated with saltpeter (potassium nitrate) on the inside. The idea was simple: Put white wine into the antimonial cup at, say, 6 p.m., and by 6 a.m., the saltpeter would have rendered said wine into an emetic (if it wasn't already).

After taking the wine, the patient would, in all likelihood, vomit as if vomiting had once been in style but suddenly was on the wane. If vomiting did not begin, the patient would try again. But careful, oh young sickling of the premedical era: You could also die! From vomiting too much. As if offering consolation, many antimonial cups of this era were produced bearing the following inscription: "You are a wonder of nature and for all people a certain cure."

DANDELION WINE

Four quarts of dandelions. Cover with four quarts of boiling water; let stand three days. Add peel of three oranges and one lemon. Boil fifteen minutes; drain and add juice of oranges and lemon to four pounds of sugar and one cup of yeast. Keep in warm room and strain again; let stand for three weeks. It is then ready to bottle and serve.

—From *Old-Time Recipes for Home Made Wines, Cordials and Liqueurs* by Helen S. Wright, 1922

Dandelion Wine

OUR RECIPE

MAKES 1 GALLON (3.8 L)

3 to 4 quarts (3 to 4 kg) lightly packed
 dandelion heads, greens removed
3 cups (600 g) sugar
Zest and juice of 2 oranges
Zest and juice of 2 lemons

1 cup (240 ml) fresh orange juice, at
 room temperature
2 tablespoons grated peeled fresh ginger
1 package (0.2 ounces/5 g) wine yeast
1 teaspoon yeast nutrient

Sanitize all equipment prior to beginning.

- Put the dandelion heads in a large bowl and cover with water. Squish or muddle the heads around, removing any dirt or bugs. Take the heads from the water and place them on a clean kitchen towel, then remove any green parts from the heads and place the heads in a stockpot.

- Add 2 quarts (2 L) water and bring to a boil. Reduce the heat to low and simmer for 5 to 10 minutes, then remove from the heat. Once cooled, cover the pot and steep the heads for 3 days.

- After steeping, strain the mixture through a fine-mesh strainer lined with cheesecloth, pressing on the solids to extract as much liquid as possible. Discard the solids. Return the liquid to the stockpot and add the sugar, zests and juices from the 2 oranges and 2 lemons, and the ginger. Bring the mixture to a boil, then reduce the heat to a simmer and cook, stirring occasionally, for 20 minutes.

- Pour the mixture into a sanitized 2-gallon (7.5-L) fermenting bucket and add enough water to make 1 gallon (3.8 L). Let cool to room temperature.

- While cooling, pour the 1 cup (240 ml) orange juice into a clean 1-pint (480-ml) jar. Stir in the wine yeast and yeast nutrient. Cover and let sit for 1 to 2 hours, until the yeast is activated and bubbling.

- Add the orange juice–yeast mixture to the dandelion mixture in the fermenting bucket. Cover and seal the fermenting bucket with an air lock and ferment for 2 to 3 days.

- Rack the liquid into a sanitized 1-gallon (3.8-L) glass jug and seal with an air lock. Let the wine ferment for 6 to 9 months before bottling and drinking.

DRINK UP!

It takes a certain kind of person to pull off a wine spritz, or a "sangaree" as it was known by our forefathers, with style, but if you have that kind of person in your life, hold them close and never let them go. For it's also true that this person truly knows how to relax.

QUINCE WINE SPRITZ
SERVES 1

Imagine walking into a pub and ordering a Quince Wine Spritz. This is why cookbooks will prevail.

¾ cup (180 ml) Quince Wine
(see recipe, page 72)
½ ounce fresh orange juice
1¼ cups (300 ml) soda water

Dash of Orange Bitters (see recipe,
page 151)
Orange wedge, for garnish

Pour the quince wine and orange juice into a tall glass full of ice. Top with the soda water and Orange Bitters. Garnish with the orange wedge.

DANDELION WINE COCKTAIL
SERVES 1

As a footnote to our earlier recipe, a bit of trivia. Wikipedia produces the following disambiguation for dandelion wine:

- *Dandelion Wine*, a 1957 novel by Ray Bradbury
- *Dandelion Wine*, a 1997 Russian TV-movie based on the novel
- Dandelion Wine, a folk music band/duo based in Canada
- Dandelion Wine, a musical duo based in Melbourne, Australia
- "Dandelion Wine," a song by Blackmore's Night from their 2003 album *Ghost of a Rose*
- "Dandelion Wine," a song by Ron Sexsmith from his 2004 album *Retriever*
- "Dandelion Wine," a song by Gregory Alan Isakov from his 2009 album *This Empty Northern Hemisphere*

There must be something to it!

¼ cup (60 ml) Garden Gin (see recipe,
page 167)
½ cup (120 ml) Dandelion Wine
(see recipe, page 79)

½ ounce Lemon Shrub (see recipe, page 131)
Splash of soda water
Lemon wedge, for garnish

In a cocktail shaker full of ice, combine the Garden Gin, Dandelion Wine, and Lemon Shrub. Shake until chilled and strain into a rocks glass full of ice. Top with the soda water and garnish with the lemon wedge.

SACK POSSET
SERVES 6 TO 8

Recipes for various possets date back to medieval times, from whence it originated as a medicinal beverage and was made in every variety imaginable, from lemon to treacle. At the base, all possets are made the same way: Hot milk curdled with wine or what have you, spiced and flavored with whatever is on hand. This Sack Posset is ambitious, blending eggs, sherry, milk, and cream, plus spices. It's not unlike those cake-in-a-cup drinks the person in front of you at Starbucks is always ordering.

3 whole eggs
6 egg yolks
1 cup (240 ml) dry sherry
3 cups (720 ml) milk
1 cup (240 ml) heavy cream
½ cup (100 g) sugar

½ teaspoon ground cinnamon
¼ teaspoon ground mace
Pinch of salt
¼ teaspoon freshly grated nutmeg
   or ground cinnamon

- In a large heatproof bowl, whisk together the whole eggs, egg yolks, and sherry until well blended. Place the bowl over a saucepan of gently boiling water, making sure the water does not touch the bottom of the bowl. Continue to whisk until the mixture is warmed through, 5 to 7 minutes.

- In a separate saucepan, combine the milk, cream, sugar, cinnamon, mace, and salt and heat just until the mixture comes to a boil.

- Very slowly add the hot milk mixture to the egg mixture, whisking continuously to avoid curdling the eggs. Whisk until frothy. Ladle into heatproof glasses and serve garnished with nutmeg or cinnamon.

SHERRY SANGAREE
SERVES 1

We know, we know: Phonetically, "sangaree" is to sangria as "sammich" is to sandwich —anyone over five years old who utters the name sounds like a fool. Still, there are differences between the two. In this one, a house red is substituted for a dry sherry; in colonial times, sangaree would have featured port or Madeira. And a sammich would have obviously been squirrel meat. (Just kidding. Maybe.)

2 ounces (60 ml) dry sherry
1 ounce Ginger Liqueur
   (see recipe, page 168)
½ ounce honey

Pinch of ground nutmeg or ground mace
Pinch of salt
1 strip lemon peel, for garnish

CHAPTER IV

In a small cocktail shaker full of ice, combine all the ingredients except the lemon peel. Shake until well chilled and strain into a cordial glass. Garnish with the lemon peel.

RUBY SANGAREE

SERVES 1

. . . and here we have your port-based sangaree; this one is an altogether heavier affair.

3 ounces (90 ml) ruby port
½ ounce fresh orange juice
½ teaspoon superfine sugar

Pinch of freshly grated nutmeg
Pinch of salt
1 strip orange peel

In a small cocktail shaker full of ice, combine all the ingredients except the orange peel. Shake until well chilled and strain into a cordial glass. Garnish with the orange peel.

BLACK AND BLUE VELVET

SERVES 1

And finally, a deep cut from the Alannah Myles catalog, this one for the Bluecoats.

½ ounce Blueberry Syrup (see recipe, page 129)
½ cup (120 ml) champagne or other dry sparkling wine

2 ounces (60 ml) stout beer

Pour the Blueberry Syrup into the bottom of a champagne flute. Slowly pour the champagne over the syrup; do not mix. Place a barspoon with its back side up over the flute and slowly pour over the stout to float the beer on top of the champagne.

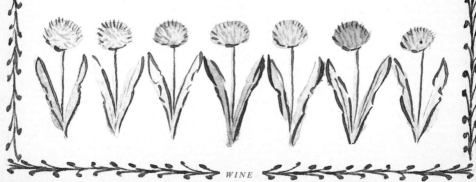

TWO COBBLERS: RED AND WHITE

When colonists realized they had neither the supplies nor the tools to properly make the traditional (and often meaty) suet puddings they'd enjoyed on the other side of the Atlantic, the cobbler was born. These were a sweeter, somewhat lighter affair, with fruit flavors being at the core. Cobblers were traditionally made from a base spirit (most popular was sherry), sugar, fruit, and citrus (acid). Since shrubs contain sugar, fruit, and acid, we'll use them here to create these modern interpretations. Do use dry wines, and depending on your taste when it comes to sweet things, you may want to dial up the amount of shrub to taste.

RED COBBLER
SERVES 1

½ cup (120 ml) red wine, preferably dry, such as Cabernet Sauvignon or Merlot
¾ ounce Strawberry Shrub (see recipe, page 131)

Crushed ice
1 to 2 strawberries, thinly sliced, for garnish

In a cocktail shaker full of ice, combine the wine and shrub and shake until chilled. Strain into a rocks glass full of crushed ice and garnish with the sliced strawberries.

WHITE COBBLER
SERVES 1

½ cup (120 ml) white wine, preferably dry, such as Sauvignon Blanc or Pinot Grigio

¾ oz Cucumber Shrub (see recipe, page 131)
Crushed ice
Thinly sliced cucumber, for garnish

In a cocktail shaker full of ice, combine the wine and shrub and shake until chilled. Strain into a rocks glass full of crushed ice and garnish with the sliced cucumber.

GEORGIAN PEACH
SERVES 1

We have reflected in this book, perhaps to an unpatriotic degree, on both Jefferson's and the nation's failures during our first (though some would say continued) attempts at making wines that might be worth a damn. Giving deference to politeness, let us consider something (one of the many things) Jefferson did successfully manage to produce: peaches.

For this luxurious concoction, we simply ask that you use your learnings thus far in this book to accentuate the positive.

1 ounce peach puree
1 ounce Spiced Rum (see recipe, page 113)

3 ounces (90 ml) chilled Quince Wine
(see recipe, page 72)
Splash of chilled soda water

In a champagne flute, combine the peach puree and Spiced Rum. Add the quince wine and top with the soda water.

ICEHOUSE SLOSH
SERVES 4

As you might imagine, spoilage of food and drink alike was a major concern in colonial times, and any technological progress made in the ongoing fight was greeted with the fervor that accompanies new Apple product releases today—to the degree that, for some, ice itself became a sort of fetish object. How do we make it? How can we keep it? What fine beverages may I put it in?

Among the pre-refrigeration fanboys was none other than George Washington himself, who marveled as the wealthiest families in Philadelphia began to build homes with pre-electricity "ice houses" dug into their basements. After careful study of the ice houses of friends, Washington constructed his own at Mount Vernon in the mid-1780s, based directly on the one that still sits underground at Sixth and Market in Philadelphia, just paces from the Liberty Bell.

2 cups (480 ml) red wine, preferably
dry, such as Cabernet Sauvignon
or Merlot

¼ cup (60 ml) Chocolate Syrup
(see recipe, page 129)
Pinch of salt
Whipped cream, for serving, optional

- In a bowl, combine the wine, Chocolate Syrup, and salt and mix until blended. Pour the mixture into a shallow baking dish and place in the freezer. Every 30 minutes, use a fork to break up the mixture as it freezes. Continue this process until the mixture is frozen, about 2 hours.

- Before serving, scrape the frozen mixture with a fork into a slush. Top with whipped cream, if desired.

CHAPTER V

RUM & PUNCH

IT CAME FROM 'CANE & WAS QUITE ABLE

It's 1650, and the humble minister Increase Mather—father of Cotton Mather, who'd go on to infamy presiding over the Salem Witch Trials—has been driven to distraction. Rum has overtaken Boston. With nearly the same quickness as a viral breakout among the new and now quickly growing population, rum—a crudely distilled liquor first imported from the West Indies and then made even more crudely in New England—has insinuated itself into daily life at an astonishing clip.

Rum is cheap. Rum is easy to produce. Rum is strong enough to peel the paint off a wall. Rum is essentially the crack of the 1600s, with the notable difference being that everybody likes it. Well, almost everybody. As rum becomes a cheap salve, social menace, and ceremonial drink alike and, for a time, as good a currency as legal tender, Increase Mather looks upon his congregation and sees what sober preachers for hundreds of years henceforth will see: A mind-altering substance ripping straight through his community.

There's naught, no doubt, so much the spirit calms as rum and true religion.

—Lord Byron

"'It is an unhappy thing,' he writes, 'that in later years a Kind of Drink called Rum has been common among us. They that are poor, and wicked too, can for a penny or two-pence make themselves drunk. [. . .] They are addicted to this vice and thus incapable of temperance.'"

—From *Customs & Fashions in Old New England* by Alice Morse Earle, 1893

Love the rum though we may, Mather was not wrong. If our colonial days were punctuated by the intake of beer and ale, the nights of many colonials were marked by rum. And whether you're talking about rum's accidental invention, the fortunes it made for men, the lives it ruined, or its place in the political sphere, this much is true: In rum, we see a microcosm—the original sin, if you will—of American vice.

WHAT IS RUM?

Put ever so simply, rum is the gasses of molasses. Put less simply, rum is—or at least, was—a dirty, toxic, mongrel brew whose potency and pungency may have been the most nastily appropriate response ever to the world of the royalty whose harsh demands inadvertently oversaw its creation. And that creation has a timeline that somewhat mirrors that of the early days of these United States.

Just as the British Crown was investigating what spoils could be reaped from the North American Continent, so too were the English engaged in a campaign of exploitation in the West Indies. (To put it mildly, America ultimately fared better in the long run.) After colonials failed grandly at producing any number of would-be worthwhile crops in Barbados—including what was generally agreed upon at the time to be the worst tobacco produced anywhere in the world—they finally struck gold in producing sugarcane in the early 1600s. And with that, a boom was born: The population of Barbados swelled in the first half of that century from high double digits to high quintuple digits. Entrepreneurs, indentured servants, slaves, and outright criminals flocked to the islands accordingly.

And while various versions of a liquor distilled from sugarcane runoff had appeared elsewhere throughout human history (usually at the hands of alche-

mists searching for various cures), it's fair to say that rum as we know it today originated in these islands. Only, it wasn't rum at first: It was called kill-devil, a name descriptive enough that one need not say much more. When it was ultimately revealed to be lucrative indeed, a sort of seventeeth century–style rebranding effort saw it transition to rumbullion (a hybridization of British and Gypsy slang), and from there, in short order, to rum.

And it was something more crude than we can really imagine today. Its process is redolent of what you'd imagine prehistoric trailer park meth would have been like. Here, in broad strokes, is the idea:

In the process of refining sugar, the sticky, viscous remains cure themselves over time into molasses, the gunk of preindustrial times.

Molasses, as it turns out, will ferment if you leave it (along with whatever other sugar-process scum you might have) rotting in the riotous Barbadian heat for days on end.

After the resulting sludge has been laid out long enough, thereby producing an unholy, nasty ooze, you can then mix it with water, citrus, and spices, and run it through a jerry-rigged, highly dangerous, 1600s-era distillation process one to three times.

And then you can age it, or not. Either way, the resulting potable is so insanely strong that, if injected into one's urethra (as some did endeavor to do), it would cure your syphilis.

The rum of today, of course, has had many of those old wrinkles ironed out. Indeed, a chic marketplace has arisen for aged rums à la whiskey, with flavors as complex as those revered in Scotch or bourbon. But upon its introduction in the West Indies and shortly thereafter in the American colonies, rum was nothing short of a phenomenon that transformed life as our forefathers knew it. For better or for worse.

Maladies Believed to Be Cured by Kill-Devil, Rumbullion, or Rum

- Syphilis
- Death, by three more minutes with which to express one's final wishes
- Excess of yellow bile (common in the tropics)
- Lower gastrointestinal disturbances (but, conversely, could cause "the dry gripes")
- Scurvy (bleeding gums, sore joints, loose teeth, non-closing wounds)
- Malaria
- Minor ailments in children
- Death by drowning (maybe)

THE PUNCH BOWL

If the spirit of rum itself was vice, the punch bowl it was served in represented nothing so much as community. Well, for those who could afford it, at least. The working poor of colonial days by and large drank their rum neat; the upper classes, however, preferred punch as its very origins traced directly the great heights of the British empire. For punch didn't come into the world fully formed, you see, but as a descendant of *paantsch*—the Hindi word for "five," in this case being a drink made of five ingredients: spirit, sugar, lemon, water, and tea—discovered by Anglos while beating the Indian subcontinent into submission as they plundered India's tea in the 1600s.

But if punch was a stolen idea, the punch bowl was the innovation on top of it, and its tendency toward extravagance represents the closest rummies ever got to Keats's Grecian urn. Punch bowls were inscribed to commemorate events; they were given as gifts; they were ostentatiously presented as displays of personal wealth and generosity. One of them even happens to be something you beer drinkers will know as the Stanley Cup. And in the rum era, it went down like this: A plain old bottle of rum would have had the same stigma as street drugs. But punch was completely about status.

And in punch, and the punch bowl, we also see the roots of the modern cocktail. But that would be a ways off.

THE TUN TAVERN & 1775 PUNCH

Taverns, as we've noted, can contain many different lives, certainly over years and often within the same moment. What is one customer's scene of the crime, a location marred by a particularly shameful night, can also be another's totem of romance. Opened in 1686 in Philadelphia, just paces from the Delaware River, the Tun Tavern—or Peggy Mullan's Red Hot Beefsteak Club, as it was known when Franklin, Jefferson, and Washington drank there (really)—contained more history than most.

Serving as an incubator for any number of organizations, militias, and secret societies for almost a century, the Tun Tavern birthed the U.S. Marine Corps and can take responsibility for the founding of the Masons, too. It led a hundred lives, and dark, pernicious rum flowed through them all. The Tun was built just in from a wharf by the Carpenter family with lucre they'd earned in Barbados during previous years. Some bars have reputations, but what the Tun had eclipses the very idea of rep. So many of the beams that gird American life were forged here that it was flat-out historic. So much so that a replica of it stands today—not in Philadelphia, but at the National Museum of the Marline Corps near Quantico, Virginia: The original Philly location burned down in 1781 and the site rests under what is now highway I-95. If that's not America, my friend, I do not know what is.

And in Quantico, as in Philadelphia, they serve 1775 Punch, which is said to be based on an original recipe from the year the Marines were founded there. Think of 1775 Punch this way: It's where the ancient navy grog meets hip-in-1775-and-2016 punch. Or, if you will, an American grog: the old grog that warded off scurvy at sea. This one destroys morals, memory, and other diseases that plague the landlubber.

✕✕✕

From a U.S. Marine Corps student handout on history, customs, and courtesies, the following describes the conduct during a Mess Night, when the traditional rum punch is brought forth:

Mess President:

"THE FLOOR IS NOW CLOSED FOR TOASTING. MR. VICE, BRING FORTH THE RUM PUNCH."

The stewards give each marine some rum punch that is made from four parts dark rum, two parts lime juice, one part maple syrup, and a small amount of grenadine, and chilled with ice. When everyone has their glasses charged the president says:

Mess President:

"IN 1776, ONE OF THE FIRST RECRUITING POSTERS ORDERED RECRUITS UPON ENLISTMENT 'TAKE COURAGE THEN, SEIZE THE FORTUNE THAT AWAITS YOU, REPAIR TO THE MARINE RENDEZVOUS, WHERE IN A FLOWING BOWL OF PUNCH, AND THREE TIMES THREE, YOU SHALL DRINK.' LONG LIVE THE UNITED STATES AND SUCCESS TO THE MARINES. MR. VICE, A TOAST TO THE CORPS AND COUNTRY."

Mr. Vice:

"MARINES, A TOAST: LONG LIVE THE UNITED STATES AND SUCCESS TO THE MARINES."

Members of the Mess:

"LONG LIVE THE UNITED STATES AND SUCCESS TO THE MARINES."

NOTE: *After this, the members drain their glasses of rum punch and place them on the table upside down. At one time, marines are reputed to have given this toast while standing with one foot on their chair and one foot on the table. As an interesting footnote, the Jacobites in England and Scotland, who did not recognize the current monarch of England, performed the loyalty toast by raising their glasses over a bowl or a finger bowl of water to symbolize that they were toasting the "true king over the water" (i.e., in exile in France). Some of them even did this during the coronation banquet of George III. As a result of this, finger bowls were banned from English royal banquets until 1905. A tradition that has passed into disuse is the one of breaking the glass after the traditional toast by either throwing the glass over the left shoulder or by snapping the stem of the glass with the fingers (specially made "toasting glasses" with 1/16-inch (2-mm) diameter stems were made for this purpose). The glass was broken so that "no lesser of a toast could be drunk" from the glass.*

The entire mess then remains standing and sings all three verses of the "Marines' Hymn." When finished, the president announces, "LADIES AND GENTLEMEN, PLEASE JOIN ME IN A ROUND OF APPLAUSE FOR THE SNCO CLUB STAFF WHO PREPARED AND SERVED THE MEAL IN HONOR OF OUR MESS NIGHT." The mess president then leads the applause. After recognizing the club staff, the president asks, "LADIES AND GENTLEMEN, WILL YOU JOIN ME AT THE BAR?"

1775 Punch

OUR RECIPE

SERVES 18 TO 24

With all due respect to today's jarheads, many contemporary recipes for 1775 Punch favor a sickly sweet pineapple juice as the dominant flavor. How this happened we can't say, exactly—the original called for grenadine instead. But in the interest of compromise, here we present an alternate route, taking cues from the East and incorporating make-your-own spiced tea with lime and ginger as well. And yes, pineapple juice, too.

2 limes, thinly sliced
4¼ cups (1 L) gold rum
2½ cups (600 ml) pineapple juice

1¼ cups (300 ml) fresh lime juice
6 cups (1.4 L) Spiced Black Tea
(see recipe, opposite)

- Arrange the lime slices on the bottom of a Bundt pan. Fill the pan with water to cover the slices and freeze until solid.

- In a 1-gallon (3.8-L) container, combine the rum, pineapple juice, lime juice, and tea. Cover and chill until cold.

- Transfer the chilled mixture to a punch bowl and add the frozen lime ice ring.

- Serve the rum punch in glasses full of ice.

Spiced Black Tea
MAKES 6 CUPS (1.4 L)

½ cup (110 g) packed brown sugar
2 tablespoons loose black tea

1 piece fresh ginger, peeled and
thinly sliced

In a medium saucepan, combine 6 cups (1.4 L) water and the brown sugar and bring to a boil. Remove from the heat, add the tea and ginger, cover, and steep for 20 minutes. Strain and cool.

And Now, Some Notes on Rum and Hedonism Through Time

There is a continuous line of a type of man—the arc of dude, the concept of it, if you can bear it—that runs from Rabelais and Philip, First Duke of Wharton, on through to Keith Richards and Bill Murray. Bawdy men, these. Hungry for what we will politely call "experience." Rakes, they once called them: a term so insidiously perfect we completely forgot to keep using it. (Sidebar: Can we begin to again?)

That man is a part of the story of rum, too.

At the core of rum's spiritual aura—the spirit's spirit, if you will—is a hedonism that persists to this day. Born in the oppressive heat of the tropics, built for revolt from both God and man, rum is sensual through and through. Comparatively, whiskey is a blunt object; vodka, cold and utilitarian; gin, bracing and mean hearted. But rum? Rum is made for indulgence.

And while we've made much of rum at what today would be called the street level, rum was born in a time in which, among the ruling class, there existed a privileged subculture whose primary purpose was the pleasures of the flesh.

The London Hellfire Club, for instance, began in 1718 when the aforementioned Duke Philip found the then so-called respectable houses of entertainment wanting. What Philip wanted was more entertainment. And so there began a series of

DO WHAT THOU WILT

clubs that polluted the lands first, and then the popular imagination, with a concept of hedonism so extreme that the jury is still out as to whether it crossed the line into outright paganism or even satanism. Aleister Crowley was a member; but then, Ben Franklin himself showed up once or twice, too. We're talking *Eyes Wide Shut* stuff here, folks. And although the scant historical record suggests Hellfire members preferred port and claret, they shared an era with rum, and their tenets trickled down to the common man—most notably in their motto: "DO WHAT THOU WILT."

Here's Renaissance thinker François Rabelais, from the novel that begat the Hellfire Club's motto:

"All their life was spent not in laws, statutes, or rules, but according to their own free will and pleasure. They rose out of their beds when they thought good; they did eat, drink, labour, sleep, when they had a mind to it and were disposed for it. None did awake them, none did offer to constrain them to eat, drink, nor to do any other thing; for so had Gargantua established it. In all their rule and strictest tie of their order there was but this one clause to be observed,

Do What Thou Wilt;

because men that are free, well-born, well-bred, and conversant in honest companies, have naturally an instinct and spur that prompteth them unto virtuous actions, and withdraws them from vice, which is called honour. Those same men, when by base subjection and constraint they are brought under and kept down, turn aside from that noble disposition by which they formerly were inclined to virtue, to shake off and break that bond of servitude wherein they are so tyrannously enslaved; for it is agreeable with the nature of man to long after things forbidden and to desire what is denied us."

In recorded history, groups like the Hellfire Club first see action in the early 1700s, when Lord Wharton got his groove back. But the vibe may be eternal. After authorities shut down the first Hellfire, reincarnation began to appear, with ever more escalating extremes of secrecy, throughout the United Kingdom. Later, it lived on through the tavern keepers of Philadelphia, who inscribed its motto on their mugs. It appeared again in Hollywood, in the early film era with the likes of John Barrymore soaking in rum and sunshine, creating a legend that persists today. This vocation to loucheness creates the target audience for the Mafia. It gives us its lord and son, Frank Sinatra. And it continues in my home, tonight, quietly, as we speak.

Rum, like all great parties—and the punch bowl itself—is also aspirational.

RUM, SLAVERY, PIRACY
& OTHER BAD THINGS

Distasteful though it surely is to all but the most disgusting of modern racists, rum played a large part in the dastardly shape of colonial commerce that you may remember from grade school as "triangular trade." The idea was this: Between exporting the king's filthy lucre (in the form of crops, goods, and gold) to England, the capture and importing of slaves from West Africa, and the import/export of necessary goods to and from the colonies, both Caribbean and American, there existed an ecosystem on the back of which American commerce was born. And much misery besides.

And as it was in the streets, so too it was at sea: Rum stood at the center of it all. Rum was traded for slaves, and vice versa. Rum kept sailors going, physically and spiritually. And rum, of course, brought piracy. So much so that, unlike, say, wine, little documentation on the rise of rum exists due to incessant theft from and attacks upon its purveyors both on land and at sea. Throughout the seventeenth and eighteenth centuries, there was little record of the day-to-day production of the stuff that wasn't looted, lost, or destroyed.

Taking all this into account, it's no wonder that rum's history, like the pirates who so notably swilled it, isn't so much history proper as it is outlaw myth. And it is that myth that accounts for America's longstanding obsession with the antihero. Could there have been a Billy the Kid without rum and piracy? Could there have been gangster movies? Could there have been gangster rap?

Sure, there could have been, but it wouldn't have been the same. Rum is, as they say, the O.G.

The Brown Family

Here, your author has an ax to grind regarding the nature of American hypocrisy, commerce, race relations, and the self-regard of the North. That hypocrisy rests in the exemplar of the New England Brahmin. Have you ever wondered how they all got so rich while retaining clean hands, free from the stain of slavery? Here is your answer: They didn't.

Take, for perhaps the most notable example, the Brown family of Providence, Rhode Island. Driven by four brothers—Nicholas, Moses, John, and Joseph—the family's initial businesses were farming and shipping, but so successful were they in these endeavors that by the time of the American Revolution, the Browns had assembled a large portfolio of going concerns. In particular, John Brown's involvement in the triangular trade—itself a New England commonplace, as the area had a deep interest in producing its own rum—placed him with a heady mix of job titles, from slave trader to philanthropist to munitions manufacturer.

And with that mix came one of the more curious lives of the era. On one hand, you could choose to view John Brown as a most active Federalist and, in some ways, a major instigator in the Revolutionary War: As one of America's first military contractors, he built the first ship for the American Continental Navy. On another hand, he was a slave trader, who also put on his payroll any number of privateers (who were essentially for-hire pirates). On still another, he was a philanthropist and educator who, along with his likewise slave-trading brother Nicholas and vocal abolitionist brother Moses (with whom John fought bitterly) and astronomer brother Joseph, was very much involved in the establishment of Brown University, initially known as The College in the English Colony of Rhode Island and Providence Plantations.

The havoc wreaked by such conflicting storylines plays out in this way: John Brown, elected official and captain of industry though he may have been, was also the first American to be tried and convicted under the Slave Trade Act of 1794; for his crimes, he was sentenced to, well, no time at all, actually. He did have to give up his boat, though. Meanwhile, Brown University is still among America's most prestigious schools and yet continues to grapple with its namesake's legacy and the degree to which the institution itself benefited from the slave trade.

Cognitive dissonance: a New England speciality!

FISH HOUSE PUNCH

There's a little place just out of town,
Where, if you go to lunch,
They'll make you forget your mother-in-law
With a drink called Fish House Punch.
—An eighteenth-century verse

On the muddy banks of the Schuylkill River in Philadelphia during the Colonial era, there stood a tavern and fishing club called the State in Schuylkill. Whatever else was achieved there—fish stories, no doubt, and grievances, too—the State's lasting contribution to society then and now was Fish House Punch. It is divine.

Fish House Punch is refreshing. It's light on the palate, and yet it has the power to knock even the most stout historical figure on his/her posterior. And as it happens, it is what we mean when we say punch, but seldom receive.

One quart of Lemon Juice
One quart of Brandy
Five quarts of Rum
Five pounds of Sugar
Nine pounds of Water and ice, i.e., 4 ½ quarts

Method: Dissolve the sugar in one pint of water. Strain the lemon juice and add it to the dissolved sugar. (To make a perfect punch the rind of the lemons should be taken off to prevent the oil getting into the punch.)

There add the Rum and Brandy, with 2 quarts of water. Let this mixture be made very thorough by frequent stirring. (There remains ¾ quarts of water and ice or about 5 lbs of ice.)

continued

Reserve a portion of this mixture into a pitcher with which to strengthen and refresh later. Put about 3 lbs of ice in the bowl and in ¾ of an hour the punch is ready.

When the punch is getting low or has weakened by the dissolved ice, add the reserve mixture from the pitcher with the remaining few pounds of ice.

This makes about 2–4 gallons of punch. For a moderate family tipple, one-fourth the quantity may be enough.

—From Dr. William Camac, Governor of the State in Schuylkill,
Fish House Punch manuscript, Philadelphia, ca. 1873

Fish House Punch

OUR RECIPE

SERVES 18 TO 24

The very word *punch*, you see, is derived from the Hindi word *paantsch*, which means "five." That number refers to the original number of ingredients called for here: alcohol, sugar, lemon, water, and tea/spices. The addition of our Spiced Simple Syrup lends depth and warmth. As this is a potent drink, ice is an important ingredient, too. As it melts, it dilutes the punch and makes for easy drinking. For style points, we also include instructions on how to make an ice ring with lemons and peaches that floats on the punch. You're welcome. Enjoy.

2 lemons, thinly sliced
2 peaches, thinly sliced
1 quart (960 ml) white rum
2 cups (480 ml) brandy

1 cup (240 ml) peach brandy
2 cups (480 ml) fresh lemon juice
1½ cups (360 ml) Spiced Simple Syrup
(see recipe, page 106)

- Arrange the lemon and peach slices in a Bundt pan, alternating them in the bottom of the pan. Fill the pan with water to cover the slices and freeze until solid.
- In a 1-gallon (3.8-L) container, combine the rum, brandy, peach brandy, lemon juice, and Spiced Simple Syrup. Cover and chill until cold.
- Transfer the chilled mixture to a punch bowl and add 6 cups (1.4 L) water and the ice ring.
- Serve in glasses full of ice.

Spiced Simple Syrup

MAKES ABOUT 3 CUPS (720 ML)

2 cinnamon sticks, crushed
3 star anise pods
4 cardamom pods, crushed
5 whole cloves

6 black peppercorns
½ teaspoon salt
¾ cup (150 g) granulated sugar
¾ cup (165 g) packed brown sugar

- In a small pan, lightly toast all the spices over medium heat until fragrant, 3 to 5 minutes.

- Transfer the spices to a saucepan with both sugars and 1½ cups (360 ml) water. Bring to a boil, reduce the heat to low, cover the pan partially, and simmer for 15 minutes.

- Remove from the heat and cool. Strain the syrup and discard the solids.

- Store in an airtight container in the refrigerator for up to 3 weeks.

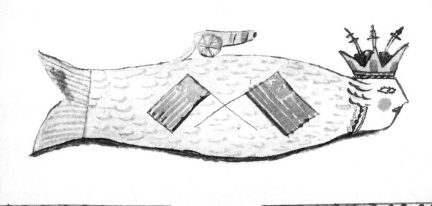

THE HANGOVER

Like any other form of mass psychosis, rum was a social fever that couldn't help but break, eventually. The British tendency toward taxation without representation would see to it that taxes were placed on the importation of molasses so steeply as to strangle the New England distilling industry that relied upon it. That tendency, of course, led to the Revolutionary War, which would make getting drunk a concern secondary to the survival of man and country alike. The aforementioned Slave Trade Act, and more like it to follow, would throw a wrench right into the heart of triangular trade. Increase Mather's call for temperance would segue into Cotton Mather's flat-out, witch-hunting intolerance (and with him perhaps the invention of America's religious right). So by the mid-1800s, America's love affair with rum would come to something of an end; we'd become a more sober land.

Or at least, we pretended to be.

DRINK UP!

Centuries after rum first caught on like wildfire in these colonies, it is mainly rum's more aspirational qualities that remain with us today. Only the most badass among us will hit the stuff straight out of the bottle, but as these syllabubs, punches, and grogs show, rum's place in the pantheon of celebration beverages is immovable.

Everlasting Syllabub
SERVES 4 TO 6

It is at this time that we feel compelled to point out that, although this book does include a number of recipes that will produce edible food, it is by no means a complete, suggested diet. If it were, you'd be living on chicken stock, some jellies and jams, and, for dessert, this syllabub, which bears the dual distinction of being 1) one of the more boozy whipped cream–adjacent things you're likely to encounter (not unlike a posset), and 2) one of the very first "cocktails," if you will, with documentation going back to the 1500s. None other than witness-to-history Samuel Pepys himself grooved hard on these.

⅓ cup (65 g) sugar	2 ounces (60 ml) dry sherry
Zest and juice of 1 lemon	2 cups (480 ml) heavy cream, very cold
¼ teaspoon salt	4 to 6 strips lemon peel, for garnish

- In a small bowl, combine the sugar, lemon zest and juice, salt, and sherry. Stir until the sugar dissolves. Let the sherry mixture sit at room temperature for 1 hour.
- In a large bowl, beat the cream until stiff peaks form. Fold in the sherry mixture until just incorporated, taking care not to overmix.
- Refrigerate until ready to serve. Garnish with the lemon peel.

Ben Franklin Milk Punch
SERVES 8 TO 10

How can it be, within the pages of this tome, that the words "excess" and "Ben Franklin" have not yet appeared in the same sentence? I'm glad we've cleared that matter up. As for the excess in this milk punch, we're afraid it was born of necessity back in colonial times: As the milk curdles, it apparently "washes" the brandy, making what was then an all-too-often dicey spirit ingestible.

6 lemons, or more if needed	½ cup (100 g) sugar
3 cups (720 ml) brandy	1½ cups (360 ml) whole milk
1 whole nutmeg, grated, or 2 teaspoons ground nutmeg	

- Peel the lemons with a paring knife or vegetable peeler and drop the peel into a 1-quart (960-ml) jar. Add the brandy, then seal the jar and let it sit at room temperature for 24 hours.
- Juice the lemons (6 lemons should yield about 1 cup/240 ml of lemon juice; juice more if necessary to reach that amount). Store the juice in an airtight container in the refrigerator until needed.

continued

- Strain the brandy into a 2 quart (1.9-L) pitcher; discard the lemon zest. Add the lemon juice, 2 cups (480 ml) water, the nutmeg, and the sugar; stir to combine.
- In small saucepan, heat the milk over medium-high heat just to a boil, stirring frequently to avoid scorching.
- Add the hot milk to the pitcher of brandy and stir to combine. The mixture will curdle immediately. Let the curdled mixture sit, undisturbed, at room temperature for 2 hours.
- Line a funnel or fine-mesh strainer with a coffee filter. Strain the curdled mixture in three to four batches into another container, discarding the curds and changing the coffee filter between batches as needed.
- Bottle the strained mixture, seal tightly, and refrigerate. Serve very cold.
- The punch will keep for up to 6 months in the refrigerator.

MARTHA WASHINGTON'S RUM PUNCH
SERVES 4 TO 6

When he wasn't drinking his own punch, Franklin was apparently a big fan of Martha's rum punch recipe.

¾ cup (180 ml) fresh lemon juice
¾ cup (180 ml) fresh orange juice
¾ cup (180 ml) Spiced Simple Syrup
  (see recipe, page 106)
¾ cup (180 ml) dark rum

1 cup (240 ml) golden rum
½ cup (120 ml) orange curaçao
Orange slices, for garnish
Lemon slices, for garnish
Freshly grated nutmeg, for garnish

- In a large pitcher, combine the lemon and orange juices, simple syrup, both rums, and the orange curaçao. Stir to combine. Keep the mixture at room temperature for about 1 hour.
- Serve in punch glasses full of ice. Garnish with orange and lemon slices and nutmeg on top.

NOTE: *This is a strong punch; serving it at room temperature over ice is necessary to slightly water the punch down.*

Hot Buttered Rum

SERVES 4 TO 6

You may have picked up on the fact that very few of the recipes you're reading here have survived into modernity—that is, until this very book single-handedly kicked off a nationwide craze for Cock Ale, Ass's Milk, and Everlasting Syllabubs. Why, nowadays you can't walk into any discotheque in America without some MBA student spilling his Quince Wine Spritzer all over you. But what's right is right, and so we must give credit where it's due: Hot Buttered Rum was always with us, having survived the centuries mainly through its presence throughout the holiday season, year in and year out. The recipe that follows here is as traditional as it comes.

1 cup (225 g) packed brown sugar, preferably dark
½ cup (115 g) unsalted butter, at room temperature
½ cup (120 ml) heavy cream
1 teaspoon ground cinnamon
¼ teaspoon freshly grated nutmeg

¼ teaspoon ground cloves
¼ teaspoon salt
1 cup (240 ml) dark rum
1 tablespoon vanilla extract
2 cups (480 ml) boiling water
Cinnamon sticks, for garnish

- In a heatproof pitcher, combine the brown sugar, butter, cream, spices, and salt. Mix until well blended and smooth. Add the rum, vanilla, and boiling water. Stir until the sugar dissolves and the butter melts.
- Serve immediately in heatproof mugs or glasses, garnished with cinnamon sticks.

Winter Grog

SERVES 6 TO 8

Another wassailing favorite, this winter grog is one of those great standbys that even outlasts the holidays. This one has warmed many a winter night. It even has the power to make rum drinkers out of previously boring individuals.

1 (1-inch/2.5-cm) piece fresh ginger, peeled and thinly sliced
3 cinnamon sticks
12 whole cloves
12 whole allspice berries
½ whole nutmeg, grated, or 1½ teaspoons ground nutmeg
2 cups (480 ml) unsweetened cranberry juice

2 cups (480 ml) apple cider
½ cup (120 ml) fresh clementine or orange juice
½ cup (100 g) sugar (see Note)
½ teaspoon salt
2 cups (480 ml) golden rum
4 clementines, peeled and sliced into wheels, for garnish

continued

- Bundle the ginger, cinnamon sticks, cloves, allspice, and whole nutmeg, if using, in a piece of cheesecloth and tie off with butcher's twine to make a sachet.

- In a large stockpot, combine the cranberry juice, apple cider, clementine juice, and sugar, along with the spice sachet and ground nutmeg, if using. Bring the mixture just to a boil over medium heat, partially cover the pot, reduce the heat to low, and simmer for 20 to 30 minutes.

- To serve, Pour 2 ounces (60 ml) of rum into a heatproof glass or mug and top with the warm cranberry-apple grog. Garnish with the clementine slices.

NOTE: *Omit the sugar if using sweetened cranberry juice.*

ROSÉ ROSE SYLLABUB WITH STRAWBERRIES
SERVES 4 TO 6

More evidence that modern life is indeed rubbish: Today, we have Cool Whip. But once, there was this:

*3 cups (375 g) fresh strawberries, hulled
    and sliced
½ cup (100 g) sugar
2 ounces (60 ml) rosé wine*

*Splash of Rose Water (see recipe, page 159)
2 cups (480 ml) very cold heavy cream
¼ teaspoon salt*

- In a medium bowl, combine the strawberries and ¼ cup (50 g) of the sugar, stirring until the berries are coated with the sugar. Let the strawberry mixture sit at room temperature until the berries release their juices and become syrupy, about 1 hour. Store the strawberry mixture in the refrigerator until ready to serve.

- In a separate medium bowl, combine the rosé wine, Rose Water, cream, salt, and remaining ¼ cup (50 g) sugar and beat until the cream forms stiff peaks. Refrigerate until ready to serve.

- To serve, divide the sugared strawberries among coupe glasses and top with the rosé rose syllabub.

Spiced Rum

MAKES ABOUT 3 CUPS (720 ML)

Q: *Once there was plain rum, how long was it before someone came up with the idea of spiced rum?*

A: Immediately following the first time someone drank plain rum.

This is not empirically true, but you get the idea. And while the business of "spicing" rum often fell to someone making more than one bottle, it's still important for you to get the tactile experience of what that was like for the colonial reseller or bootlegger. As rum hit the streets of places like Boston, leaving chaos in its wake, rum production took on a kind of ad hoc, kitchen-sink flair, with locals attempting to put their own stamp on a product that often started out with a kind of universal sameness. It was rum, it came from cane, and it could peel the paint off of a wall and replace it with chest hair.

Our at-home recipe includes neither paint nor hair of any kind, but innovation is the American way. We're sure you'll find your muse.

12 cinnamon sticks
12 whole cloves
12 whole allspice berries, cracked
6 cardamom pods, cracked
3 star anise pods

1 (1-inch/2.5-cm) piece fresh ginger, peeled and thinly sliced
Zest of 1 orange
1 vanilla bean, split lengthwise, seeds scraped
1 (750 ml) bottle golden rum

- In a small saucepan, combine the cinnamon, cloves, allspice, cardamom, and star anise and toast over medium-high heat just until fragrant, about 2 minutes.

- Transfer the spices to a 1-quart (1-L) jar with a tight-fitting lid. Add the ginger, orange zest, vanilla bean and seeds, and rum to the jar. Seal the jar and store in a cool, dark place for 2 weeks, shaking the jar daily.

- Strain the mixture through a fine-mesh strainer lined with cheesecloth, or a couple coffee filters, into a clean jar or bottle. Store, tightly sealed, at room temperature for up to 2 months.

COLUMBI

SERVES 1

Christopher Columbus allegedly discovered the pineapple on his second trip to the Caribbean and brought it back to Europe. It became a symbol of great wealth. In the colonies, the pineapple was an emblem of welcome and hospitality. According to legend, a pineapple speared on a sea captain's fence post was a beacon to friends and family, letting them know he was home safe and that they should come to eat, drink, and hear tales of his adventures.

2 ounces (60 ml) Spiced Rum (see recipe,
  page 113)
3 ounces (90 ml) pineapple juice

¼ cup (60 ml) fresh orange juice
½ ounce Cherry Shrub (see recipe, page 131)
Sliced fresh pineapple, for garnish

In a cocktail shaker full of ice, combine the rum, pineapple and orange juices, and shrub. Shake until blended and strain into a tall glass full of ice. Garnish with the sliced pineapple.

BUMBO

SERVES 1

For the most part, bumbo was grog minus the citrus element, for sailors on shorter excursions who needn't concern themselves with fighting off scurvy. In citrus's stead, you'd have sugar, nutmeg, cinnamon, and so on. But as time wore on, the lines between one man's grog and another man's bumbo began to blur. (For instance, we've been known to concoct a piping hot grog made principally from the combined ingredients of the Naval Grog and Bumbo recipes presented in these pages: Put 'em both together, bring them just shy of a boil, and serve in a coffee cup. Is it grog? Is it bumbo? Who cares!)

But for the most strict palate-based and historical interpretation, look here and find the landfaring rum concoction that made America great again for the first time ever. For it was on land that rum, via bumbo, made perhaps its most lasting mark on American politics: Politicians loved to hand it out on the campaign trail. George Washington was particularly noted for using this technique. His papers state that he used 160 gallons of rum to treat 391 voters to bumbo while campaigning for the Virginia House of Burgesses in July 1758.

2 ounces (60 ml) Golden Rum
1 ounce chilled water
2 teaspoons sugar

Freshly grated cinnamon stick, for garnish
Freshly grated nutmeg, for garnish

In a rocks glass, combine the rum, water, and sugar and stir. Garnish with a couple grates of cinnamon and nutmeg. This is traditionally served neat; however, one or two cubes of ice can be added.

Traitor

SERVES 4

Like we were saying: Add to bumbo a spot of citrus and warm it up and you're well on your way to Naval Gro—I mean, TRAITOR!

How dare you sully your bumbo.

¾ cup (180 ml) gold rum or Spiced Rum
   (see recipe, page 113)
¾ cup (180 ml) fresh orange juice

2 tablespoons honey
¼ teaspoon freshly grated nutmeg

In a small saucepan, combine all the ingredients and gently warm over medium-low heat, stirring frequently—do not bring to a boil. Serve in heatproof mugs or glasses.

Blackstrap

SERVES 1

The variations abound, you see. Taking all of the above in, we invite you to take on the Grog/Bumbo/Traitor/Blackstrap conundrum as a challenge to come up with your own, and name it accordingly. Ever had a piping hot cup of Grasse's Revenge? Buddy, you should live so long.

2 ounces (60 ml) golden rum
1 ounce blackstrap molasses (see Note)

Soda water
Lemon or lime wedge, for garnish

In a tall glass, combine the rum and molasses and stir until the molasses is dissolved. Fill the glass with ice and then top with the soda water. Stir to combine and garnish with the lemon or lime wedge.

NOTE: Blackstrap molasses has a very robust, dark, bitter flavor. For a lighter version, substitute light molasses, baking molasses, or Ginger Molasses Syrup (see recipe, page 129).

Chapter VI

Temperance Drinks

TEMPERANCE: THE BAD IDEA THAT WOULDN'T DIE

When most of us think about the American temperance movement, our thoughts turn to the era of Prohibition, and that makes sense. For it was there that the American abstainer had both its greatest victory and its final defeat. This is because it was a terrible idea. We are Americans, and we were born to drink. Without it, would there be jazz? No. Country music? Not on your life. Rock 'n' roll? How could you even ask! Nor would there be the lion's share of American literature, movies, advertising, and, well, we could go on. America's most lasting empire and contribution to humanity has been popular culture. And it's hard to imagine how any of it would have happened without booze.

Prohibition may have articulated the moral beliefs about drinking of some, but for *all* Americans, it ushered in a wave of organized crime and deeply damaging political graft that persists in one form or another to this day.

Keep your head cool with Temperance, your feet warm with exercife, rife early and go soon to bed; and if you are inclined to get fleshy, keep your eyes open and mouth shut.

—Benjamin Franklin, *Poor Richard's Almanack* (1732–1758)

Like so many other pieces of legislation that have, over our history, sought to regulate human behavior—whether it be our ways of cutting loose or even our ways of loving—it was doomed from the start.

But the temperance movement in America is in fact older than America. It began with the very first colonial settlers here—the aforementioned Puritans, who sought to live a sober lifestyle from the very start. (But even they were not averse to, say, a cider here and there. Multiple times daily.)  As a religious conviction, of course, this is fine and indeed very good for those who choose to believe in it and practice it. But what about everybody else?

Everybody else in early America, pretty much, liked to drink—as we have discussed, early and often, throughout the day.

And as the colonies gained momentum and the populace that came with it grew—all colored by the influx of rum and the attendant hard lives of those times—even the most proud alcoholic would have to admit that by as early as the mid-1600s, booze was already becoming a problem. Within a decade of the Crown's edict for the colonies to establish taverns as community hubs, their officers were seeking solutions to a growing problem of rampant public drunkenness. The English asked, "How are we supposed to make these people do what we want when they're so loaded all the time?" When, in the due course of time, some of those same taverns became the war rooms of revolutionary forces, they had to deal with more of the same. To which they in turn asked, "How are we supposed to make these people do what we want when they're so loaded all of the time?"

Viewed through that prism, the various temperance movements in America have always been about a political and/or religious structure attempting to manage personal behavior. And in this, man has always failed. But given what we know about the average man's daily intake in those days, who could blame a power structure clamoring for some sense? While the question of temperance and sobriety was certainly in the air as the Puritans first touched American soil, for the sake of argument, let's go back to Increase Mather.

Even though—as we noted in the last chapter—Mather was not *wrong* about the ruin

rumbullion was bringing to men and their families in the colonies, this is not to say he was always *right*, either. To wit, he vehemently opposed legislation outlawing discrimination against Catholics, but advocated that all Jews be converted to Protestantism. He, as a matter of course, used his pulpit directly for political gain. He believed in and warned others of an angry, vengeful God, not just from his post but also in the form of more than a hundred texts published throughout his lifetime, on everything from how earthquakes were evidence of God's wrath to the famous jeremiad he published defending the Salem Witch Trials. He had disdain for a great many things—even fancy dress did not escape his judgment —but more than anything, he hated booze. If his style rings a bell, that's not surprising: In his way, he may well have been America's very first arch conservative, stoking culture wars for his own purposes.

Mather's concerns would echo down through America's first two hundred years, culminating in the Volstead Act (the National Prohibition Act), and may have been the first wedge issue in American politics. And as sobriety went in and out of fashion among one group or another over the decades, a more practical question loomed: What the hell are we supposed to drink instead of booze?

To that end, much human endeavor was expended on trying to find drinks—any drink, really—that went down as well as a good stiff one. But here is the heart of the matter: As well-intentioned as these innovators might have been, all of their creations tasted a hell of a lot better when you put some of that ever-loving booze in them.

It is to the temperance movement's misguided but valiant efforts that we dedicate this chapter; here, we'll discuss how to make stuff that doesn't have booze in it, but will be that much better when you do put booze in it.

WHO'S WHO AMONG THE BORING: AMERICAN TEMPERANCE NERDS

Increase Mather
First New England preacher to call for temperance in the wake of rumbullion!

Dr. Benjamin Rush
A signer of the Declaration of Independence who penned *An Inquiry Into The Effects Of Ardent Spirits Upon The Human Body And Mind.*

Rev. Lyman Beecher
Charter member of the Connecticut Moral Society, with a mission to fight off "Sabbath-breakers, rum-selling tippling folk, infidels, and rugg-scruff."

THE DRUNKARD'S PROGRESS

TEMPERANCE DRINKS

RHUBARB WINE

To each gallon of juice add one gallon of soft water, in which seven pounds of brown sugar have been dissolved. Fill a keg or a barrel with this proportion, leaving the bung out, and keep it filled with sweetened water as it works over until clear; then bung down or bottle as you desire. These stalks will furnish about three-fourths their weight in juice, or from sixteen hundred to two thousand gallons of wine to each acre of well cultivated plants. Fill the barrels and let them stand until spring, and bottle, as any wine will be better in glass or stone.

—From *Old-Time Recipes for Home Made Wines, Cordials, and Liqueurs*
by Helen S. Wright, 1922

Strawberry Rhubarb Lemonade

OUR RECIPE

Initially discovered by the Chinese in antiquity and used for its medicinal properties—all associated with the digestive system—rhubarb found its way to Europe and the American colonies by the 1700s. By the middle of the century, this ancient vegetable, known for its tartness, would enjoy a sudden vogue; consider it the kale of the 1750s. And though reports vary regarding the plant's first appearance on the American scene, no less than Ben Franklin himself was responsible for sending one variety of seeds on to pioneering Philadelphia botanist John Bartram, claiming it to be the "true rhubarb," said to be from the Great Wall of China. In any case, once it was here, colonials couldn't get enough of rhubarb tarts and pies. And like that pesky kale, it'd eventually find its way into everything—including this lemonade.

STRAWBERRY RHUBARB LEMONADE

SERVES 1

Rhubarb adds increased flavor and tang to the lemonade. The Strawberry Rhubarb Syrup can also be poured over ice cream, yogurt, or pancakes.

¼ cup (60 ml) fresh lemon juice
2 ounces (60 ml) Strawberry Rhubarb
*   Syrup (see recipe, below)*

1 cup (240 ml) still or sparkling water

- In a tall glass, combine the lemon juice and Strawberry Rhubarb Syrup; stir.
- Fill the glass with ice and top with the still or sparkling water.

STRAWBERRY RHUBARB SYRUP

MAKES ABOUT 2 CUPS (480 ML)

1½ pounds (680 g) rhubarb, chopped
1 pound (455 g) strawberries, hulled and
*   chopped*
½ cup (100 g) granulated sugar

½ cup (110 g) packed brown sugar
Zest and juice of 1 lemon
½ teaspoon salt

- Combine all the ingredients in a saucepan and add 1 cup (240 ml) water. Bring to a boil. Reduce the heat to medium-low and simmer, stirring frequently, until the rhubarb has become tender, about 20 minutes.
- Remove from the heat and strain the syrup through a fine-mesh sieve, pressing on the solids to extract as much liquid as possible.
- Store the syrup in an airtight container in the refrigerator for up to 2 weeks.

Chocolate, Coffee & Tea

Considering tea's great import in the story of America's birth—the leafy beverage serving a totem for the taxation without representation that brought us both the event of the Boston Tea Party and, much later, the essentially incoherent political movement of the 2000s—the historical record suggests that our colonial friends weren't as hot on the beverage as you might think. For one, it was expensive; for another, those who'd emigrated from England may well have not even been in the habit of drinking it anyway, as tea's dominance of that country wouldn't hit its apex until America was nearing independence. (Perhaps the Brits got into tea as a way of consoling themselves after the big breakup. Like one does.) For some early Americans, tea was such an exotic import that they didn't even know what the hell to do with it: One report from Salem during this era details how tea leaves would be salted, buttered, cooked, and eaten, with the resulting liquid discarded. (When your narrator learned of this, he was embarrassed for our forefathers. I mean, really.)

Coffee, and its perfect soul mate, chocolate, were different stories, and both enjoyed massive popularity during this time, as they do today, but perhaps even more so. While a through-line can be drawn from then to now regarding chocolate's popularity, whether in hot liquid form or as a solid delight, coffee may well have been the most important virgin beverage of all to our founding fathers.

As taverns proliferated (and indeed, became ever more wild, unruly places), they were increasingly the province of the common man. Beginning in the mid-1600s, gentlemen and men of business alike would flock to coffee houses to do much as they do today: hold meetings, catch up on the day's events, and tweak hard on that energy-giving, life-saving bean. But even this was not simple: With coffee becoming a bona fide craze in colonial days, it too would run up against the Puritan menace.

Some thought coffee was in possession of aphrodisiac powers; others thought it inhibited procreation altogether (see our Cock Ale recipe on page 31). Either way, it was a conversation the Puritans didn't like having. A coffee temperance movement, though attempted, would gain little ground, however. Wars, embargoes, and taxes in the years to come would push tea forever to the side at the American table and establish coffee as our preference through the ages.

SWITCHELS & SHRUBS

Before there was soda, there was switchel. And before there were cocktails, there were shrubs. In the case of the former, we were probably better off for it: Switchel, at its base, is essentially water, vinegar, ginger, and something sweet. Endless variations abounded in colonial days, but one thing is for sure: Kids weren't getting fat from any of them. Meanwhile, shrubs—though also a predecessor to modern sodas in some senses—were closer to something you might have around your bar today. Altogether more sophisticated than a switchel, the shrub evolved as a sort of liquid fruit preserve designed to be mixed with water (fizzy or not, your choice) and, eventually, alcohol (finally! yay!).

The process for making shrubs is simple, and not unlike pickling in some ways. In the most general sense, what it involves is pouring vinegar over fruits or botanicals, allowing the mixture to sit for a few days, and then reducing it to a syrup capable of bringing pleasure to witch and witch hunter alike. What follows, then, are our humble suggestions for both standalone nonalcoholic refreshment as well as fine mixers with the spirit of your choosing. Just don't tell Increase.

SWITCHEL

"Mix with five gallons of good water, half a gallon of molasses, one quart of vinegar, and two ounces of powered ginger. This will make not only a very pleasant beverage, but one highly invigorating and healthful."

—From *Practical American Cookery and Domestic Economy*
by Elizabeth Hall, 1853

Switchel

OUR RECIPE

SERVES 1

¼ cup (60 ml) Ginger Molasses Syrup
(see recipe, below)

¼ cup (60 ml) apple cider vinegar

Add the syrup and apple cider vinegar to a tall glass and stir to combine. Pack the glass with ice and add 1 cup (240 ml) water. Stir and serve.

GINGER MOLASSES SYRUP

MAKES ABOUT 1 CUP (240 ML)

1 (1½-inch/4-cm) piece fresh ginger,
peeled and sliced
1½ tablespoons molasses

1 cup (220 g) packed brown sugar
½ teaspoon salt

- Combine all the ingredients in a medium saucepan, add 1 cup (240 ml) of water, and bring to a boil. Reduce the heat and simmer for 10 minutes. Remove from the heat, cover, and allow to cool.

- Strain to remove the slices of ginger. Store the syrup in an airtight container in the refrigerator for up to 2 weeks.

FLAVORED SYRUPS & SHRUBS

At the heart of all temperance drinks—those things we drank when we weren't drinking alcohol until we eventually found that they went even that much better with alcohol—were syrups and shrubs. What follows, then, is hopefully a tool kit for anyone wishing to employ their own kitchen on a journey to those times just preceding the creation of the cocktail; what you find there, we pray, is a palate with which you can let your imagination (and your home bar) run wild. Throughout these recipes, we have endeavored to use nothing but ingredients and flavors available in the eighteenth century. We wish you a safe and happy journey!

- Combine all the ingredients in a saucepan; bring to a boil, reduce the heat to low, and simmer for 20 to 30 minutes. If necessary, strain the mixture and discard the solids (see Note).
- Transfer the syrup to an airtight container and store in the refrigerator for up to 2 weeks.

NOTE: *If the recipe contains cooked fruit, it can be strained for a thinner, translucent syrup, left in, or pureed until smooth for a thicker, opaque syrup.*

FLAVORED SYRUPS
MAKES ABOUT 2 CUPS (480 ML) SYRUP PER RECIPE

Ginger Syrup

*½ cup (25 g) fresh ginger, peeled and
    sliced into ⅛-inch (3-mm) rounds*
1 cup (200 g) sugar
2 cups (480 ml) water
¼ teaspoon salt

Brown Sugar Syrup

1 cup (220 g) packed brown sugar
2 cups (480 ml) water
¼ teaspoon salt

Vanilla Syrup

*1 vanilla bean, split lengthwise, seeds
    scraped, both beans and seeds used*
1 cup (200 g) sugar
2 cups (480 ml) water
¼ teaspoon salt

Chocolate Syrup

1 cup (95 g) unsweetened cocoa powder
1½ cups (300 g) sugar
1 cup (240 ml) water
¼ teaspoon salt

Cinnamon Syrup

3 cinnamon sticks
1 cup (200 g) sugar
2 cups (480 ml) water
¼ teaspoon salt

Nutmeg Syrup

*1½ tablespoons freshly
    grated nutmeg*
1 cup (200 g) sugar
2 cups (480 ml) water
¼ teaspoon salt

continued

Strawberry Syrup

1½ cups (200 g) hulled and
quartered strawberries
½ cup (100 g) sugar
1½ cups (360 ml) water
¼ teaspoon salt

Cherry Syrup

1½ cups (300 g) pitted
and halved cherries
½ cup (100 g) sugar
1½ cups (360 ml) water
¼ teaspoon salt

Peach Syrup

1½ cups (340 g) diced fresh peaches
½ cup (100 g) sugar
1½ cups (360 ml) water
¼ teaspoon salt

Blueberry Syrup

1½ cups (190 g) fresh blueberries
½ cup (100 g) sugar
1½ cups (360 ml) water
¼ teaspoon salt

FLAVORED SHRUBS

Main ingredient (usually chopped fruit) • Sugar • Vinegar • Salt

- Mix equal parts chopped fruit of choice and sugar together; cover and refrigerate for 24 to 48 hours.
- Strain the mixture through a cheesecloth-lined sieve, reserving the syrup and any undissolved sugar that may still be in the container.
- To the syrup, add an equal amount of vinegar and 1 pinch of salt per serving and stir to combine and dissolve any remaining sugar.
- Transfer the shrub to an airtight container and store in the refrigerator for 2 to 3 weeks.

Some of our favorite fruits for making shrubs with this technique include the following:

Strawberry • Raspberry • Blackberry • Blueberry • Lemon
Watermelon • Cantaloupe • Honeydew • Cucumber • Cherry
Peach • Apricot • Nectarine • Plum • Pineapple

SHRUB COOLER

SERVES 1

Our man in the kitchen says: "This cooler is inspired by the switchel. The vinegar in your various shrubs is similar to the vinegar in switchel, and here it'll add tartness and be refreshing on a hot day."

2 ounces (60 ml) shrub of choice   *1 cup (240 ml) still or sparkling water*

Pour the shrub into a pint glass full of ice and top with the still or sparkling water. Stir to combine.

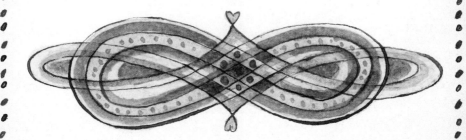

RASPBERRY SHRUB OR VINEGAR

Place red raspberries in a stone jar, cover with good cider vinegar, using about one quart vinegar to two gallons fruit, let stand two or three days, strain through a jelly bag, squeezing carefully; let stand overnight so it will become perfectly clear; measure and place on stove, and boil and skim until it boils up clear; add one pint sugar to every pint juice as just measured, and cook half an hour. Let stand till cold, then can and seal as directed in Canning Fruits. Some use one-third vinegar (one quart to two quarts fruit) but if fruit is juice the above proportions make a much finer flavored shrub. Black raspberries may be used, or strawberries, making *Strawberry Shrub*, and blackberries, using for latter only a pint sugar to one quart juice, making *Blackberry Shrub*. Some, after straining, let it simmer on back of stove two hours, while others let boil ten minutes, in either way canning when hot, but the above method has been "tried and not found wanting."

Always procure very ripe, juicy fruit. For a drink use two or three teaspoons to one glass water, according to strength desired.

—From *The New Practical Housekeeping: A Compilation of New, Choice and Carefully Tested Recipes*, 1890

Cranberry Shrub

OUR RECIPE

MAKES ABOUT 1 QUART (960 ML)

3 cups (280 g) cranberries, fresh or frozen
½ cup (110 g) packed brown sugar
½ cup (100 g) granulated sugar

¾ cup (180 ml) white vinegar
¼ cup (60 ml) balsamic vinegar
½ teaspoon salt

- Combine all the ingredients in a large saucepan with 3 cups (720 ml) water and bring to a boil. Reduce the heat and simmer, stirring frequently, until the berries pop and become tender, about 20 minutes.

- Remove the pan from the heat and cool slightly. Working in batches, puree the cranberry mixture in a food processor.

- Transfer the pureed mixture to a cheesecloth-lined sieve and strain, pressing on the solids to extract as much liquid as possible. Discard the solids (or reserve for the chutney recipe on page 134).

- Store the shrub in an airtight container in the refrigerator for up to 1 month.

CRANBERRY SHRUB SODA
SERVES 1

2 ounces (60 ml) chilled Cranberry Shrub
    (see recupe, page 133)

1 cup (240 ml) soda water

Pour the Cranberry Shrub into a tall glass full of ice. Top with the soda water and stir to combine.

CRANBERRY CHUTNEY
MAKES 3½ CUPS (840 ML)

1½ cups (360 ml) cranberry solids from
    shrub recipe (see recipe, page 133)
½ cup (75 g) golden raisins
½ cup (80 g) diced apple (peeled or not,
    depending on your preference)
¼ cup (40 g) minced red onion
½ cup (60 g) chopped walnuts, toasted

Zest and juice of 1 orange
½ teaspoon ground cinnamon
½ teaspoon ground allspice
¼ teaspoon freshly grated nutmeg
¼ teaspoon ground cloves
Salt and pepper

In a large bowl, combine the cranberry solids, raisins, apple, onion, walnuts, orange zest and juice, cinnamon, allspice, nutmeg, and cloves. Stir until well mixed. Season with salt and pepper. Store in an airtight container in the refrigerator for up to 1 week.

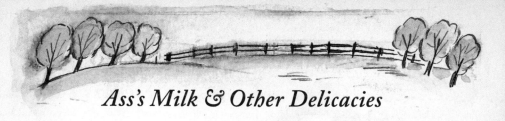

Ass's Milk & Other Delicacies

OTHER TEMPERANCE DRINKS FOR THOSE WHO DISLIKE FUN (OR, ALTERNATIVELY, CHILDREN)

Ass's Milk
Ginger Beer
Sarsaparilla
Burdock
Barley Water
Eau Sucre
Curds and Whey
Lait Sucre
Sham Champagne
Coffee with Fish Skin
Beef Tea

As high-minded—or high-handed, rather—as the long arc of any number of temperance movements were, they were also marked by a culture of denial. Like most movements (or people) who defined themselves by the things they *didn't* do, they'd painted themselves, from the start, into a corner. And when they felt the need to break out, to actually finally have a drink and feel the electric, godly jolt of alcohol, those aligned with or sworn to temperance would do a sad thing indeed:

They would try to call it medicine.

DRINK UP!

In mixed company, you won't hear it said out loud much, but there is a prejudice among those of us who love the sauce: The man who does not drink is untrustable. And while there is much to love in nonalcoholic sweet teas, shrubs, and other flavored waters, it's also true that I would never let a man who favored Artificial Ass's Milk anywhere near my daughter.

GINGER BEER

SERVES 4

Medicinal use of ginger root dates all the way back to 500 BCE, but its procession to ginger beer per se was slow and stately indeed. The first commercial production of ginger beers wouldn't happen until the early 1800s; before that, what one would have encountered would've been something less like the ginger beers or ginger ales we can pick up today and more like a wild, fresh kombucha. Try this one and see if it doesn't put a spring in your step.

¼ teaspoon champagne yeast
3 tablespoons grated peeled fresh ginger
Zest and juice of 1 lemon
¾ cup (165 g) packed brown sugar

¼ teaspoon salt
2 quarts (2 L) filtered water,
  at room temperature

- In a large pitcher, combine all the ingredients and stir until the sugar is dissolved. Transfer the liquid to a clean 2-quart (2-L) soda bottle (or divide between two 1-quart/960-ml bottles), leaving about an inch (2.5 cm) of headspace.

- Tightly screw the caps onto the bottle(s) and store at room temperature for 24 to 48 hours—the bottle(s) will become hard, like an unopened liter of soda. Transfer the bottle(s) to the refrigerator and chill before serving.

- When ready to serve, cover the bottle with a tea towel and open slowly to release the pressure.

ARTIFICIAL ASS'S MILK

SERVES 2 TO 4

Make no mistake: When we/they say "Ass's Milk," we/they mean "that milk which would be produced by a donkey." And when we/they say "Artificial Ass's Milk," we/they mean "the next best thing to that milk which would be produced by a donkey." That may sound like we're damning it with faint praise, but in our experience, it has proven best to just drink it and leave as much as possible unsaid.

2 cups (480 ml) skim milk
¼ cup (50 g) sugar

¼ teaspoon salt

In a medium saucepan, heat the milk over medium-high heat. Add the sugar and salt and stir until they have dissolved. Serve immediately.

BARLEY WATER
SERVES 6

This barley water would have been drunk like a switchel—as a hydrating beverage for field-workers. But you'll notice that its process also has a lot in common with tea, and some versions of barley water recipes are just about as old as tea, which dates back to the ancient Greeks.

1 cup (200 g) pearl barley, rinsed
Zest and juice of 2 lemons

¼ cup (55 g) packed brown sugar
½ teaspoon salt

- Put the rinsed barley and 2 quarts (2 L) water in a stockpot, cover, and bring to a boil. Reduce the heat to low and simmer for 30 minutes.

- Put the lemon zest and juice, brown sugar, and salt in a heatproof pitcher.

- Strain the barley water into the pitcher and stir until the sugar dissolves. Refrigerate until well chilled.

NOTE: *The leftover cooked barley can be saved and added to soups and salads, or used in porridge. Store in an airtight container in the refrigerator for up to 1 week or in the freezer for up to 6 weeks.*

CAROLINA SWEET TEA
SERVES 8

And here we have another one of the surviving temperance recipes, only Carolina Sweet Tea has done much better than merely surviving; it has become one of the (if not *the*) signature drinks of the American South. And over the last few hundred years, it hasn't changed much. This recipe, inspired by a couple of historic recipes we've found, swaps out the black tea you encounter throughout the South today for green tea.

¼ cup (1 g) green tea leaves
¾ cup (165 g) packed brown sugar

½ teaspoon salt

- Put the tea in a large tea infuser or wrap it in cheesecloth and tie with butcher's twine.

- In a medium saucepan, heat 1 quart (960 ml) water just until it barely comes to a boil. Remove from the heat; add the tea, brown sugar, and salt. Stir until the sugar and salt dissolve and let the tea steep for 12 minutes.

- Remove the soaked tea and pour the sweet tea mixture into a pitcher. Add an additional 1 quart (960 ml) water and refrigerate until cold before serving.

CHOCOLATE EGG CREAM

SERVES 1

Around much of the civilized world, concurrent with America's fight for independence was an ongoing interest in the restorative powers of mineral waters found in nature. And in the 1700s, enterprising chemists and scientists would begin to circle around a process by which to artificially produce those effervescent waters that so many considered a cure for an entire laundry list of ails. Little did they know that they were setting the scene for American big business in the form of the soda industry, which would come in the wake of the invention of soda water, nor could they have intuited the obesity epidemic to come on the heels of Big Soda. Well, their grandchildren would thank them, at least: for it was that 1700s discovery that also begat the soda fountain, which in turn begat the beloved Egg Cream.

½ cup (120 ml) cow's milk or Artificial Ass's Milk (see recipe, page 137)
¼ cup (60 ml) Chocolate Syrup (see recipe, page 129)

1 ounce heavy cream
Chilled soda water

In tall glass, combine the milk, chocolate syrup, and cream and stir. Slowly top with soda water. Serve immediately.

CREAM SODA

SERVES 1

Cream Soda was a creation of the soda fountain era of the 1800s—but we have it here to illustrate how close the colonials would have been to it, once soda water was on hand. Most of the original recipes would have included some combination of sodium bicarbonate, water, sugar, egg whites, and wheat flour—all but one of which would have gone into the syrup recipes then already commonplace.

1 ounce Vanilla Syrup (see recipe, page 129)
1 ounce Brown Sugar Syrup (see recipe, page 129)

Soda water

Add the syrups to a tall glass full of ice. Top with soda water and stir to combine.

GINGER BEER FLOAT

SERVES 1

Ah, but as we know, ice cream *would* have been on hand in the colonial era. And ginger beer, too! Although this is a temperance recipe, this drink greatly benefits from 2 ounces (60 ml) of Spiced Whiskey (see recipe, page 187).

½ cup (120 ml) vanilla ice cream

1 cup (240 ml) Ginger Beer
(see recipe, page 137)

Add the ice cream to a tall glass and top with the ginger beer.

CHAPTER VII

LIQUEURS, CORDIALS & MEDICINAL BEVERAGES

INDUSTRY & LUXURY

Time moves but in one direction—forward. Think of the view from your favorite stool at your favorite bar, the varieties of spirits on offer. Those spirits —the flavor profiles they feature, the history and the culture attached to their brands, the cutthroat thicket of commerce they had to go through to get there, on the other side of the bar—did not simply appear there all at once. No. Each spirit on offer to man today bears with it a long and storied journey that, by the very nature of its existence in the category of spirits, reaches all the way back to man's first sophisticated inquiries: *How do we live? How can we not die?*

Certainly if men were less ignorant, they would prefer cordial essences before crude juices, balsamic elixirs before phlegmatic waters, and mercury of philosophers before common quicksilver.

—John French, *The Art of Distillation, 1651*

All of which calls to mind nothing so much as the Greeks! Every query we have into the nature of planes, physical and otherwise, traces back to our freethinking ancient friends in Alexandria, and it is there the story of booze begins, too. Alchemy—oh, curious muddle of mysticism and ad hoc science! Has our modern world of targeted algorithms, overmedicated children, and deep-dish pizza with hot dog crust done you wrong?

For it is in antiquity that we first glimpsed the beginnings of distillation, and yea, it is across the bar tonight where we see its progress thus far. And it is still progressing. After all this time we've spent with, well, time, how curious to note that it is still moving in just that one direction, while the human mind, nevertheless the weaker vessel, can move itself all over the temporal map should it have the desire—or the aid of those spirits.

Such heady thoughts, though, would have been far out of the realm of the everyday concerns of our colonials, whose hardscrabble lives were mainly about the struggle for survival, stability, and a place to call their own. One wonders if in the whole first century of colonial settlement in America anyone even uttered the very word *luxury*. But just as America itself was evolving into view, moving in that one direction, so too were the fields of science and industry, creating the conditions to bring into view that array of spirits in bottles brown and blue and green and clear that sit before you. At first, though, those spirits were not luxury items as such, not at all.

They were designed to keep you alive.

THE APOTHECARY
& THE HOME STILL

Even as relatively late in human history as the colonial days were, Western medicine had still not advanced very much beyond the findings concurrent with the Renaissance. So if one took ill, the prognosis was almost always bad. Do you want to know how bad? Oh, you don't want to know.

I will tell you anyway, to help you see the sense in drinking. (That's what you came here for, was it not?) Even as we blazed new paths in so many other fields in the seventeenth century, much of medicinal theory still operated on the notion that the human body held four "humors": black bile, yellow bile, phlegm, and blood. Thus, it was the job of the

doctor—such as the "doctor" was in those days—to observe the patient, figure out which of said humors was out of whack, and provide treatment to adjust the imbalance. Which could mean inducing vomiting or diarrhea, or, yes, bloodletting or—the most popular option—the doctor merely acting like he was doing something when in fact he was just waiting around to see if you died or not. A lot of the time, you'd just die.

As time wore on, two key things happened: Western Europe's ongoing exploration and exploitation of other parts of the world put us in touch with other cultures and new strains of plants and herbs (well, new to us, anyway), and, taking inspiration from the ancient alchemists and putting both this new knowledge and plant life to use, the apothecary came to replace ancient medicine. Like the scientific walk in the dark that preceded it, much of what came out of the apothecary was questionable. But its most lasting contribution lives with us today on the racks of every bar in the land that's worth its while in the form of bitters.

Bitters were first known as elixirs and come to us in a wide variety of flavors, but loosely speaking, they're all essentially the same: herbs, spices, and other natural ingredients preserved in alcohol. As time wore on, certain elixirs would become essential, taking on the name "bitters" as they slowly but surely worked their way into kitchen cabinets, family know-how (Grandma always recommended them for stomach trouble), and so on. Their role one day as an accessory to the cocktail would become inevitable.

But that wouldn't be for quite some time. In the colonies, as you might imagine, apothecary and the practice of medicine alike was taken up on an ad hoc basis. Your village apothecary would have most likely been an autodidact—or at best, one who'd had a bit of schooling before he'd left the Continent. Nevertheless, that apothecary would act as the local doctor, relied upon to treat general maladies and specialist-worthy illnesses alike. Across a broad range of ailments, what the apothecaries found was that, more often than not, a particular herb or fruit, either distilled or mixed with another spirit, was the best hope they had. And that if there was hope to be had, the apothecary was going to have to whip it up himself, using a mortar, pestle, and a home still. And so he did.

Of the ART of Diſtillation

Meanwhile, the can-do DIY spirit of the apothecary would also trickle down to the common hobbyist as well as some more enterprising sorts among us. Backyard stills called limbecs would become if not a commonplace, then certainly a recognized phenomenon. And in many ways, these backyard experiments would leave their mark on American drinking, first with fruits, which would give us things like perry and applejack, and eventually with grains, where we'd see in time the development of American whiskey.

✕ ✕ ✕

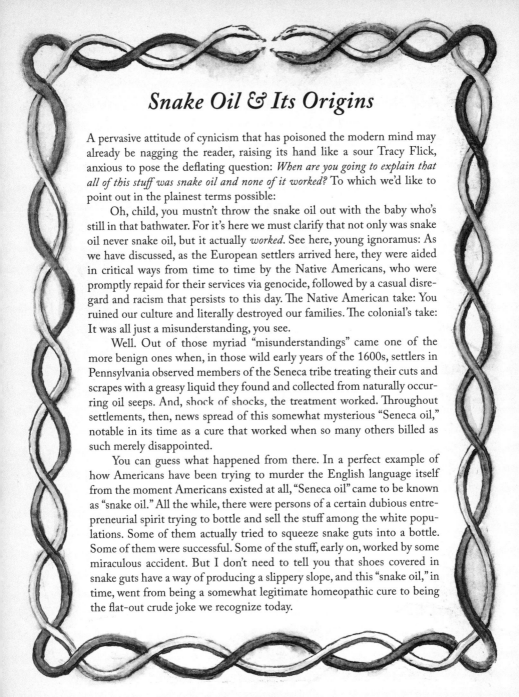

Snake Oil & Its Origins

A pervasive attitude of cynicism that has poisoned the modern mind may already be nagging the reader, raising its hand like a sour Tracy Flick, anxious to pose the deflating question: *When are you going to explain that all of this stuff was snake oil and none of it worked?* To which we'd like to point out in the plainest terms possible:

Oh, child, you mustn't throw the snake oil out with the baby who's still in that bathwater. For it's here we must clarify that not only was snake oil never snake oil, but it actually *worked*. See here, young ignoramus: As we have discussed, as the European settlers arrived here, they were aided in critical ways from time to time by the Native Americans, who were promptly repaid for their services via genocide, followed by a casual disregard and racism that persists to this day. The Native American take: You ruined our culture and literally destroyed our families. The colonial's take: It was all just a misunderstanding, you see.

Well. Out of those myriad "misunderstandings" came one of the more benign ones when, in those wild early years of the 1600s, settlers in Pennsylvania observed members of the Seneca tribe treating their cuts and scrapes with a greasy liquid they found and collected from naturally occurring oil seeps. And, shock of shocks, the treatment worked. Throughout settlements, then, news spread of this somewhat mysterious "Seneca oil," notable in its time as a cure that worked when so many others billed as such merely disappointed.

You can guess what happened from there. In a perfect example of how Americans have been trying to murder the English language itself from the moment Americans existed at all, "Seneca oil" came to be known as "snake oil." All the while, there were persons of a certain dubious entrepreneurial spirit trying to bottle and sell the stuff among the white populations. Some of them actually tried to squeeze snake guts into a bottle. Some of them were successful. Some of the stuff, early on, worked by some miraculous accident. But I don't need to tell you that shoes covered in snake guts have a way of producing a slippery slope, and this "snake oil," in time, went from being a somewhat legitimate homeopathic cure to being the flat-out crude joke we recognize today.

A Cure for What Ails You

Although the colonials, the historical record shows, treated them abhorrently, the Native Americans weren't the only ones looking to folk remedies in the absence of hard medical knowledge. In fact, the colonials were using the same methodology in attempting to gather from nature that which existing science was unable to provide. And over time, a laundry list of concoctions—based on experiences in the New World coupled with folk wisdom from the old countries—developed. In many cases, certain pairings were believed to be favorable in treating very specific conditions. Among them were these cures presented below. Each of them bears a stunningly common theme: Flavored booze will get you through.

RHEUMATISM
Prickly Ash bark subsumed in brandy

CONSUMPTION
Branches of Beaver Tree with rum or brandy

JAUNDICE
Black Cherry bark with rum, wine, brandy, or cider

INDIGESTION
Hops

CONSTIPATION
Beer made from peas

COUGH
Wood Sorrell berries with rum and brown sugar

ASTHMA
Sulfur dissolved in rum

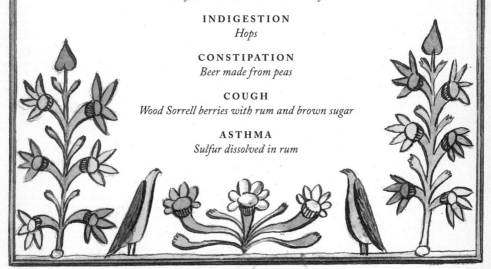

ORANGE BITTERS

Orange Peel, 1 ounce; citron peel, 1 ounce; gentian root, one half ounce.

Macerate the sliced and bruised ingredients for a week in one pint of diluted alcohol; filter or transfer to a percolator and add sufficient diluted alcohol to obtain one pint of liquid.

—From *A Treatise on Beverages, or The Complete Practical Bottler*
by Charles Herman Sulz, 1888

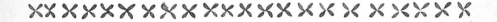

Orange Bitters

OUR RECIPE

MAKES 2 CUPS (480 ML)

1 cup (240 ml) vodka (the highest proof available) or grain alcohol

Zest of 3 oranges

1 tablespoon bitter orange peel (available in specialty stores or online)

3 cinnamon sticks, crushed, or 1½ teaspoons ground cinnamon

1 cup (240 ml) Bitters Base (see recipe, page 152)

- In a 1-pint (480-ml) jar with a tight-fitting lid, combine the vodka, orange zest, bitter orange peel, and cinnamon. Be sure all the dry ingredients are submerged in the alcohol. Seal the jar and store in a cool, dark place for 7 to 14 days, shaking the jar daily.

- Strain the orange solution into a clean 1-pint (480-ml) jar, discarding the solids. Seal the jar and store at room temperature until ready to use.

- To make the finished bitters, blend the orange solution with the Bitters Base and bottle it.

Bitters Base
MAKES ABOUT 1 CUP (240 ML)

1 cup (240 ml) vodka (the highest proof
available) or grain alcohol
1 tablespoon dried gentian root

1 tablespoon dried wild cherry bark
1 tablespoon dried quassia
1½ teaspoons dried wormwood

- In a 1-pint (480-ml) jar with a tight-fitting lid, combine all the ingredients. Be sure all the dry ingredients are submerged in the alcohol. Seal the jar and store in a cool, dark place for 5 to 7 days, shaking the jar daily.
- Strain the solution into a clean 1-pint (480-ml) jar, discarding the solids. Seal the jar and store at room temperature until ready to use.

NOTES:

- *Creating separate solutions for the Bitters Base and the orange aromatics allows for better control of flavor, as the aromatics take longer to infuse in the alcohol. An equal blend of the two is merely a suggestion; feel free to blend the base and aromatics to personal taste.*

- *Regarding the grain alcohol, using a higher proof means more flavor can be extracted from the ingredients. Using stronger alcohol can also decrease how long the ingredients steep. If you're using 190-proof spirits, check the Bitters Base after 3 days and the orange solution after 5 days. Once the base and orange solutions are infused, dilute each with equal parts water to reduce the proof to something that is safe to consume. (If you're using high-proof vodka, there is no need to the dilute solutions except for personal taste.)*

- *Orange bitters are great in cocktails or club soda, but a couple of splashes can also elevate simple lemonade and add complexity to chocolate-based recipes (e.g., frostings, cakes, or brownies).*

WHAT WE TALK ABOUT WHEN WE TALK ABOUT CORDIALS, LIQUEURS & MEDICINALS

Today, regulations exist about what is and what is not medicine, as though the mere labeling of an elixir can grant or take away its power. But tell me: Was, say, the young man in the Jamestown of the 1600s who was suffering a life-threatening fever brought back to life from the brink of said fever with the aid of a sip of usquebaugh any less properly medicated than his equivalent today with a bottle of NyQuil?

Even the most decorated modern physician will tell you that it's hard to say how much belief—faith in medicine or otherwise—plays in a patient's recovery. But when it's there, it certainly doesn't hurt. So it went with the aura attached to these spirits, and so it still goes today, in varying degrees, depending on what culture one comes from and one's own personal beliefs.

But this much we know about cordials, liqueurs, and medicinals, or whatever you would like to call them: They were all pretty much the same thing—distilled alcoholic beverages imbued with the essence of fruits, herbs, spices, or botanicals. Geographical appellations varied, but basically if you were drinking one in the pursuit of better health, you would likely have called it a cordial. If you didn't care—whether you were already in good health or past the point of caring—it was a liqueur. If you were growing up on the East Coast in the 1980s and breaking into your parents' liquor cabinet for the first time, you might have only known it as schnapps, and you deserved whatever you got. May God have mercy on your soul.

Don't Drink the Wood-er*

Much of what we talk about in this book represents one success story or another in the annals of American ingenuity—how our enterprising spirit endeavored to put booze where there was no booze, or not enough booze, before. And as charmed as our forefathers were in this regard, with even their failures with wine being at the very least instructional, there were also experiments that turned out not just as failures but altogether deadly. Buried deep in Mackenzie's *Five Thousand Receipts in All the Useful and Domestic Arts*—a sort of all-purpose how-to tome published in 1825—is the following recipe, sitting like a landmine amid Peach Brandy and Kirsh Wasser:

Alcohol from Wood

The wood is reduced to coarse saw-dust; in this state it is dried up to a temperature of 212 degrees, so as to . . .

. . . and so on. But for your own safety as well as our own—we want to liberate you, not litigate with you—this is as much of the recipe as we will reprint here. You see, as the home still and knowledge of distillation in general became more common, especially in the colonies where DIY was most often the only option for achieving a wide array of human desires, it did come to pass that certain desperate types would endeavor to make booze from wood. Results, from the start, would have been dicey. In fact, more than dicey. Deadly. In 1661, the Irish-English chemist Robert Boyle put a fine point on exactly why: Alcohol from wood was not a spirit, but methanol. As in gas. Fuel. And so on. And under no circumstances should it be consumed.

This book is all about us telling you things, the sharing of knowledge and recipes. This is something that we love to do. Knowledge of all kinds should never be hoarded; information was meant to be shared; it wants, the saying goes, to be free. So let us be free with this, then: No matter what you do, no matter what rapturous delight this book may send you into, flush'd with the desire to create spirits . . .

> . . . just don't try to make or drink booze that is made from fucking wood. You will die. Or worse.

And for the most part, this advice was heeded long before us, way back in those colonial times. Could it have been just good sense, or could it have been that wood was a more precious commodity than anything else that could have been distilled? Maybe a little bit of both. But where something is known, something will be acted upon, and indeed, people did make booze from wood. For the most part, it was a rare occurrence . . . up until Prohibition, when suddenly it was ubiquitous and ruinous. Bootleggers with murder and profit in their hearts would pass it off as other spirits—and deaths from its consumption became an epidemic for a time. Once in the system, these methanol spirits would take their time—up to a week—dissembling the body's functions until, slowly, the consumer would perish. The worst part? Other than dying, I mean?

You'd never taste the difference.

> *Here in Philadelphia, we live in a constant state of danger in this regard, as "wooder" is the common pronunciation of "water."*

PLEDGE THAT YE USE THIS BOOK IN CONCORDANCE WITH JOHN FRENCH'S *THE ART OF DISTILLATION*

Seeing as how the story of cordials and liqueurs is generally one of evolution —where folk remedies met pseudoscience and, stymied for want of real, provable success stories, decided to have a party—there are few heroes. But John French, whose quotation began this chapter, is without a doubt one of them. Published in London in 1651, at the height of a burgeoning transcontinental distillation wave, was French's *The Art of Distillation*. It would have been one of the most widely used how-tos of the age by those on either side of the Atlantic who had an interest in making their own spirits. And French's salty personality comes through, even to today's reader.

But he was more than just flip. He was a fearless explorer of the world of spirits. He attempted to cure gout by making a spirit from human skulls. He came up with a cure for jaundice made by, ironically, distilling the urine of young drunkards. He sought to cure scurvy by mixing horse dung and white wine left out in the sun. He was not to be trifled with. And there was little he wouldn't try in the service of his passion.

By his own account, French saw himself as an exasperated truth teller, surrounded by contemporaries who either hoarded knowledge or passed off inferior product. This galled him every bit as much as it does us, and it's for this reason and others that we ask you to rise now—be it in your kitchen or shed or nearest public library—and take what amounts to no less than the pledge offered by French himself in *The Art of Distillation*:

I   Surely, there is matter enough for philosophers, and also some philosophers at this day for the matter, although they are unknown to us. There are, says Sendivogius, without doubt many men of a good conscience both of high and low degree (I speak knowingly) that have this medicine and keep it secretly. If so, let no man be discouraged in the prosecution of it, especially if he takes along with him the five keys which Nollius sets down which indeed all philosophers with one consent enjoin the use and observation of.

II Seeing it is a divine and celestial thing, it must be sought for from above, and that not without a full resolution for a pious and charitable improvement of it.

III Before you take yourself to the work, propound to yourself what you seek, and enter not upon the practice until you are first well versed in the theory. For it is much better to learn with your brain and imagination than with your hands and costs, and especially study nature well, and see if your proposals are agreeable to the possibility thereof.

IV Diligently read the sayings of true philosophers, read them over again and again and meditate on them, and take heed that you do not read the writings of imposters instead of the books of the true philosophers. Compare their sayings with the possibility of nature, and obscure places clear ones, and where philosophers say they have erred, do beware, and consider well the general axioms of philosophers, and read so long until you see a sweet harmony, and consent in the sayings of them.

V Imagine not high things, but in all things imitate nature, viz. in matter, in removing what is heterogeneous, in weight, in color, in fire, in working, in slowness of working, and let the operations not be vulgar, nor your vessels. Work diligently and constantly.

VI If it is possible, acquaint your self thoroughly with some true philosophers. Although they will not directly discover themselves that they have this secret, yet by one circumstance or another it may be concluded how near they are to it. Would not any rational man that had been conversant with Bacon, and seeing him do such miraculous things, or with Sendivogius who did intimate the art to some word by word, have concluded that they were not ignorant of it? There have been philosophers, and perhaps still are, that although they will not discover how it is made, yet may certify you, to the saving of a great deal of costs, pains, and time, how it is made. And to be convinced of an error is a great step to the truth. If Ripley had been by any tutor convinced of those many errors before he had bought his knowledge at so dear a rate, he had long before, with less charges attained to his blessed desire.

ROSE WATER

Take of the leaves of fresh damask roses with the heels cut off, 6 lbs.—water, as much as to prevent burning. Distil off a gallon.

The distilled waters should be drawn from dried herbs, because the fresh cannot be got at all times in the year. Whenever the fresh are used the weights must be increased; but whether the fresh or dry are made use of, it is left to the judgement of the operator to vary the weight, according as the plants are in greater or less perfection, owing to the season in which they grew, or were collected.

—From *Five Thousand Receipts in All the Useful and Domestic Arts*
by Colin MacKenzie, 1825

Rose Water

OUR RECIPE

MAKES 2 CUPS (480 ML)

Rose water is excellent for flavoring teas, ice creams, custards, and frostings. (See our recipe for Rosé Rose Syllabub with Strawberries, page 112.)

1 cup (50 g) dried rosebuds, firmly packed (see Note)

2 cups (480 ml) boiling distilled water

- In a heat-resistant 1-quart (960-ml) container, combine the rosebuds and the boiling water and let steep for 30 minutes.
- Strain the mixture, discard the rosebuds, and bottle the rose water. Store in the refrigerator for up to 1 week.

NOTE: *Make sure the rosebuds are organic and safe for consumption. Many dried rosebuds are chemically treated and unsafe to eat. Fresh roses can be substituted in this recipe; however, they must be chemical-free and organically grown. Use 2 to 3 cups (50 to 75 g) firmly packed fresh petals.*

ROSE WATER TONER

MAKES 1 CUP (240 ML)

To use, soak a cotton ball in toner and apply to face and skin. You can also add a spoonful or two to bathwater for a fragrant treat. Store in the refrigerator in an airtight container or spray bottle for up to 1 month.

½ cup (120 ml) Rose Water (see recipe, above)

½ cup (120 ml) witch hazel

In an 8-ounce (240-ml) jar, combine the Rose Water and witch hazel.

DRINK UP!

The health claims made regarding these beverages were of such a wide variety that to survey the resulting drinks today is more like a road map of how we wound up drinking what we drink. And that, my friends, is a beautiful thing. Rosy Tipple, you live on in Hendrick's gin and cucumber! Usquebaugh, you are with us in Fernet-Branca! And on and on.

To your health!

Bitter Orange Soda Water

MAKE ABOUT 1¼ CUPS (300 ML)

We would be remiss—nay, cruel—if we walked you through this entire book about the hardest American drinking ever done without at least one solid hangover cure. This would be that (it'll also serve well those individuals who are suffering from an upset stomach).

¼ cup (60 ml) fresh orange juice
1 tablespoon sugar
Pinch of kosher salt

½ cup (120 ml) soda water
5 or 6 dashes Orange Bitters
    (see recipe, page 151)

In a tall glass, combine the orange juice, sugar, and salt; stir until the sugar and salt dissolve. Fill the glass with ice and add the soda water. Top with the Orange Bitters and gently stir to combine.

Rosy Tipple

SERVES 1

If the Rosy Tipple—which uses two of the recipes we've already shared with you—calls to mind a certain "curious" brand of gin that is "infused with rose and cucumber," well, then you've caught us. Here is a drink even more Hendrick's than Hendrick's. We suggest you try it with . . . Hendrick's.

2 ounces (60 ml) gin
1 ounce fresh lemon juice
½ ounce Cucumber Shrub (see recipe,
    page 129)

½ cup (120 ml) soda water
Dash of Rose Water (see recipe, page 159)

In a rocks glass, combine the gin, lemon juice, and Cucumber Shrub. Fill the glass with ice. Add the soda water and a dash of Rose Water to taste, then stir to combine.

USQUEBAUGH
SERVES 4

The popular but gross Goldschläger of the 1990s wasn't the first spirit to use actual gold leaf, you know. This cordial, whose name is derived from the Gaelic for "aqua vitae," would have been the first to try and capture "the sun's golden radiance" in spirit form. But there's a lot of other things going on here: mace, saffron, licorice, and so on. It's one of the more complicated cordials of the Colonial era.

½ cup (75 g) raisins
¼ cup (40 g) chopped dried figs
2 cinnamon sticks
1 teaspoon freshly grated nutmeg
6 whole cloves
½ teaspoon ground mace

1 tablespoon chopped licorice root
Pinch of saffron
3 cups (720 ml) brandy
½ cup (120 ml) Madeira or sherry
Edible gold leaf, optional

- In a 1-quart (960-ml) jar with a tight-fitting lid, combine all the ingredients except the edible gold leaf.

- Seal the jar tightly and store in a cool, dark place for 7 to 10 days, shaking the jar daily. Line a funnel or fine-mesh strainer with a coffee filter or cheesecloth and strain the mixture into a clean pitcher.

- Add the edible gold leaf, if using; stir to combine and transfer to an airtight bottle. Store at room temperature for up to 6 months.

HYSTERICAL WATER
SERVES 4

The good feminists among us will know: "Hysteria" and "hysterics" were terms used in less enlightened times to oppress women—systemic gaslighting, if you will. And while we cannot endorse this tactic or line of thinking popular in the Colonial era and stretching through to the 1800s (eventually giving us the fainting couch, which we cannot hate entirely), we will concede: Male or female, everybody goes to the zoo sometimes. This recipe seeks to be a calming stress-reducer. The original recipe for hysterical water, we kid you not, would have called for millipedes.

3 cups (720 ml) brandy
1 teaspoon dried lavender
1 teaspoon dried valerian
1 teaspoon dried St. John's wort

1 tablespoon dried chamomile
2 teaspoons dried peppermint
¼ cup (60 ml) honey

- In a 1-quart (960-ml) jar with a tight-fitting lid, combine the brandy and all the herbs. Seal the jar and store in a cool, dark place for 7 to 10 days, shaking the jar daily.

- Line a funnel or a fine-mesh strainer with a coffee filter or cheesecloth and strain the mixture into a clean pitcher. Add the honey and stir to combine.

- Transfer to an airtight bottle. Store at room temperature for up to 6 months.

RATAFIA

SERVES 4

Ratafias, to this day, are produced in France, Italy, and Spain. Quite popular in the Colonial era, they would have been made with wine endemic to those regions. But, again, times being what they were, importing these wines would have been prohibitively expensive. So here's an early American improvisation on the form using rum.

⅓ cup (35 g) finely ground coffee beans
1 cup (220 g) packed brown sugar
1 vanilla bean, split lengthwise

½ teaspoon salt
1½ cups (360 ml) gold rum

- In a 1-pint (480-ml) jar with a tight-fitting lid, combine the ground coffee and 1½ cups (360 ml) water. Seal the jar and place in the refrigerator for 12 hours to cold-brew. Strain the coffee into a 1-quart (960-ml) jar with a tight-fitting lid. Set aside.

- In a medium saucepan, combine 1 cup (240 ml) water, the brown sugar, vanilla bean and seeds, and salt. Bring the mixture just to a boil, stirring to dissolve the sugar and salt. Reduce the heat to low and simmer for about 15 minutes. Remove from the heat and cool to room temperature.

- Transfer the brown sugar–vanilla mixture to the jar with the cold-brewed coffee. Add the rum, seal the jar, and store in a cool, dark place for 3 days, shaking the jar daily.

- After 3 days, remove the vanilla bean and transfer the coffee mixture to a bottle, where it can be stored indefinitely at room temperature.

ROASTED RYE COFFEE

In *Thirty-Five Receipts from "The Larder Invaded,"* William Woys Weaver notes the following about a recipe for rye coffee from the recipe book of Samuel R. Franklin of Philadelphia (a teacher, alderman, constable, and health commissioner):

The embargo placed by President Jefferson on British Vessels in 1807 resulted in a severe shortage of imported coffee. Large numbers of Americans were forced to turn to roasted rye as a coffee substitute. For many years, even after the embargo was lifted, rye coffee was known locally as "family coffee," and because of its relative cheapness, it became a standard feature of institutional cookery.

While touring the prison at Philadelphia in 1829, the English Quaker Thomas Shillitoe noted that the inmates were served rye coffee sweetened with molasses with their breakfast rations. Rye coffee received a better name later in the nineteenth century when it was discovered that it lacked caffeine and retained some of the nutritional value of the whole grain. Certainly, it is one of the few coffees of which, if one chooses, one can eat the grounds without deleterious effect!

RYE COFFEE
SERVES 4 TO 6

2 cups (400 g) rye   Heavy cream, for serving
Molasses, for serving

- Preheat the oven to 200°F (95°C).
- Place the rye in a heat-resistant container. Boil 2 cups (480 ml) water and pour it over the rye. Let the rye steep for 7 minutes. Drain the rye in a fine-mesh sieve and rinse under cold water.
- Tamp out as much water as possible from the rye and transfer it to a rimmed baking sheet. Spread it into a single layer and place it in the oven to dry for about 1½ hours.
- Once the rye is completely dry, increase the oven temperature to 375°F (190°C) and, stirring occasionally, roast the rye for about 50 minutes.
- Remove the rye from the oven and cool to room temperature.
- To make a cup of rye coffee, grind the roasted rye in a coffee grinder. Measure 1 to 2 tablespoons ground rye per 1¼ cups (300 ml) water. Add the rye and water in a saucepan and bring to a boil; boil for 10 minutes. Strain the coffee through a fine-mesh sieve into a mug and serve with molasses and cream.

FLAVORED BITTERS

- Blend equal parts (or by taste) of the Bitters Base Mixture (see below) with one or more of the Aromatic Mixtures (see below) in a bottle with a dropper cap that's large enough to accommodate the bitters.

- Store tightly sealed at room temperature.

BITTERS BASE
MAKES ABOUT 1 CUP (240 ML)

1 tablespoon dried gentian
1 tablespoon dried wild cherry bark
1 tablespoon dried quassia

½ tablespoon dried wormwood
1 cup (240 ml) vodka (the highest proof
    available) or grain alcohol

- In a 1-pint (480-ml) jar with a tight-fitting lid, combine all the ingredients. Be sure all the ingredients are submerged in the alcohol. Seal the jar and store in a cool, dark place for 5 to 7 days, shaking the jar daily.

- Strain the mixture into a clean jar, discarding the solids. Seal the jar and store at room temperature until ready to use.

AROMATIC MIXTURES

Orange Bitters

1 cup (240 ml) vodka (the highest
    proof available) or grain alcohol
Zest of 3 oranges
1 tablespoon dried bitter orange peel
6 cinnamon sticks, crushed

Grapefruit Bitters

1 cup (240 ml) vodka (the highest proof
    available) or grain alcohol
Zest of 2 medium grapefruits
1 tablespoon fennel seeds

Lemon Bitters

1 cup (240 ml) vodka (the highest
    proof available) or grain alcohol
Zest of 3 lemons
1 tablespoon dried chamomile flowers
1 tablespoon dried lemon verbena

Maple Walnut Bitters

1 cup (240 ml) whiskey
1 cup (100 g) walnuts, toasted and
    coarsely chopped

NOTE: Once strained, add 1 tablespoon maple syrup to the walnut-infused
whiskey before blending with the base
mixture.

continued

Pecan Bitters

1 cup (240 ml) whiskey
1 cup (150 g) pecans, toasted and
   coarsely chopped
2 cinnamon sticks, crushed
½ whole nutmeg, cracked

Molasses Bitters

1 cup (240 ml) gold rum
1 tablespoon molasses

Coffee Bitters

1 cup (240 ml) gold rum
1 cup (110 g) ground coffee beans

Cherry Bitters

1 cup (240 ml) whiskey
¾ cup (80 g) cherries, pitted and halved
1 teaspoon whole cloves

Raisin Bitters

1 cup (240 ml) gold rum
1 cup (290 g) raisins
1½ teaspoon allspice berries, cracked

Chocolate Bitters

1 cup (240 ml) whiskey
1 cup (125 g) cacao nibs
¼ teaspoon red pepper flakes

- In a 1-pint (480-ml) jar with a tight-fitting lid, combine all the ingredients. Be sure all the ingredients are submerged in the alcohol. Seal the jar and store in a cool, dark place for 7 to 14 days, shaking the jar daily.

- Strain the mixture into a clean jar, discarding the solids. Seal the jar and store at room temperature until ready to use.

HERBAL TEA BLENDS

Liberty Tea

1 teaspoon dried sweet goldenrod
1 teaspoon dried peppermint

New Jersey Tea

1½ teaspoons New Jersey tea or red root
   tea leaves

Sumac Tea

1 tablespoon dried sumac berries

Soothing Tea

1 tablespoon dried lemon verbena
½ teaspoon grated peeled fresh ginger

Red Wink Tea

1 teaspoon dried chamomile flowers
1 tablespoon dried raspberry leaf

- Put the dry ingredients in a mug or heatproof glass. Pour 1 cup (240 ml) boiling water over the dry ingredients and steep until the desired strength is achieved, 5 to 15 minutes.

- Strain the mixture into a mug, discard the strained ingredients, and sweeten with honey, or brown or raw sugar, if preferred, and serve hot or cold.

GARDEN GIN
MAKES ABOUT 3 CUPS (720 ML)

One of the most delightful revelations to come from our distillery up in Tamworth, New Hampshire, was the response to our summer line of gins with all-natural infusions—our Apiary Gin in particular, infused with local honey (to say nothing of our Art in the Age SAGE spirit, which takes a similar cue). We weren't the first people to come up with a concept like this, of course—garden gin is a simple home infusion that makes the most of any herb garden. To not give this one a whirl would be positively inelegant.

Leaves from 3 sprigs of thyme, chopped
Leaves from 3 sprigs of mint, chopped
Leaves from 2 sprigs of tarragon, chopped
6 fresh sage leaves, chopped

1 tablespoon fresh lavender buds, slightly crushed
1½ tablespoons lemon zest
1 (750 ml) bottle gin

- Add the thyme, mint, tarragon, sage, lavender, and lemon zest to a 1-quart (1-L) jar with a tight-fitting lid. Add the gin and seal the jar tightly. Store in a cool, dark place for 1 to 2 weeks, shaking the jar daily.

- Strain the mixture through a fine-mesh strainer lined with cheesecloth, or a couple coffee filters, into a clean jar or bottle. Store, tightly sealed, at room temperature for up to 2 months.

GINGER LIQUEUR
MAKES ABOUT 3 CUPS (720 ML)

An ailing King Edward VII made ginger liqueur famous when his doctor prescribed it at his bedside, but as you now know, alchemists and apothecaries had been fooling around with the restorative powers of ginger in their elixirs for centuries. What no one could have predicted was that the spirit would evolve into the base for one of today's more chic, high-end liqueurs, Domaine de Canton. Here's how to make your own.

½ cup (50 g) sliced peeled fresh ginger
1 vanilla bean, split lengthwise, seeds scraped
1 cup (200 g) sugar

Pinch of salt
1 tablespoon orange zest
2 cups (480 ml) brandy

- In a small saucepan with a lid, combine the ginger, vanilla bean and seeds, sugar, salt, and 1 cup (240 ml) water. Bring the mixture to a boil, stirring to dissolve the sugar. Reduce the heat to low, partially cover, and simmer for 22 minutes. Remove from the heat and set aside.

- Add the orange zest and brandy to a 1-quart (1-L) jar with a tight-fitting lid. Add the ginger mixture and seal the jar tightly. Shake to combine and store in cool, dark place for 3 days.

continued

- Taste to determine if the flavor is strong enough. If so, strain the mixture through a fine-mesh strainer lined with cheesecloth, or a couple coffee filters, into a clean container. If not, seal the jar and continue to steep for a couple more days.
- Store the strained liqueur in a tightly sealed jar or bottle at room temperature for up to 2 months.

USQUEBAUGH FLIP
SERVES 1

From the Scottish Gaelic *uisge beatha* ("water of life"), Usquebaugh is, of course, primordial whiskey. And with this Usquebaugh Flip, we can think of nothing so much as the legendary performance of Christopher Lambert in the film *Greystoke: The Legend of Tarzan*. Why, you ask? Because this is something of the same—a beautiful savage manimal, dressed up just so, right there at your table.

2 ounces (60 ml) Usquebaugh (see recipe, page 162)
½ ounce Brown Sugar Syrup (see recipe, page 129)

1 large egg
Freshly grated nutmeg, for garnish

In a cocktail shaker full of ice, combine the Usquebaugh, syrup, and egg and shake vigorously for 20 seconds. Strain into a coupe glass and garnish with a couple grates of nutmeg.

HYSTERICAL SIDECAR
SERVES 1

Hannah Glasse made Hysterical Water famous in her day, but after all the roots and seeds and dried millipedes included in her original recipe, no one much felt like finding anything to actually do with it. We saw this as a challenge, a gauntlet left out on the table, beckoning from history. And so, here is your Hysterical Sidecar.

¼ cup (60 ml) Hysterical Water (see recipe, page 162)
1 ounce orange liqueur

½ ounce fresh lemon juice
Orange or lemon zest strip, for garnish

In a cocktail shaker full of ice, combine the hysterical water, orange liqueur, and lemon juice. Shake until chilled. Strain into a coupe glass and garnish with the orange or lemon zest.

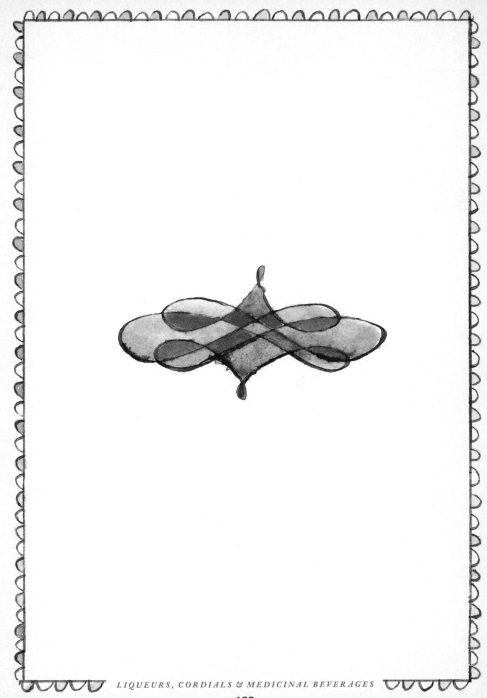

Chapter VII · V

Meanwhile, Across the Continents & the Sea

A LOOK AT SEVENTEENTH-
& EIGHTEENTH-CENTURY
SPIRITS ELSEWHERE

It is not merely snobbery, or simply Europeans being Europeans, when you hear tell of how they see us. For all that is made—and rightly so—of the American curiosity, the American friendliness, the American notion of "gumption," when our cousins across the sea look at us, they cannot help but notice that something seems to be missing. They may or may not be moved to remark upon it, but know this, fellow American friend, and know it well: When they look upon us, their eyes cannot help but be drawn to a void—the thing they believe missing from the American soul.

Call it what you will: a certain disinterest in any variables of existential funk, or maybe even a kind of proud ignorance that characterizes our politics today and indicates our already-in-progress global comeuppance. But it could just be a certain lack of sensuousness, arriving from the historical fact that Americans simply missed out on some key moments in the development of modern decadence.

Which is not to say that America is not or has never been decadent. It has been, it still is . . . to an almost admirably vulgar degree. But it's our own take on it. American decadence is unlimited mozzarella sticks. It's Sam's Club. It's binge drinking on campus. It's about volume and little else.

But true decadence, that sort of deep, languid overpleasure done with great care and cultivation, that rich indulgence that isolates one from the rest of the world to the point where all that remains is oneself and the poetics of satiety . . . well, that's something we just don't do. For better or worse, it's not really in the American psyche to go as far down the rabbit hole as J. K. Huysmans would by the tail end of the 1800s, after more than a century of Europe soaking in gin and vodka.

Now *that* was decadence. And while we fought for independence, we missed it all.

"Already, he was dreaming of a refined solitude, a comfortable desert, a motionless ark in which to seek refuge from the unending deluge of human stupidity."

—Joris-Karl Huysmans, *Against Nature*

GIN

"I . . . purchased . . . the Sign of a Cat, and had it nailed to a Street Window; I then caused a Leaden Pipe . . . to be placed under the Paw of the Cat; the End that was within had a Funnel. Customers put money in the cat's mouth and said, 'Puss, give me two Pennyworth of Gin.' I . . . put my Mouth to the Tube, and bid them receive it from the Piper under her Paw, and then . . . poured it into the funnel."

—From *The Life and Uncommon Adventures of Dudley Bradstreet*
by Captain Dudley Bradstreet, 1755

Beer Street   Gin Lane

Derived from the French *genièvre* as well as the Dutch *jenever,* terms for the natural botanical juniper berry, gin's very name checks its source. Today, variances abound, but generally speaking, gin—be it simply gin or "distilled" or "London" or what have you—is a neutral spirit that draws its central flavor characteristic from juniper. But like so many other spirits, gin has medicinal roots that trace back to alchemists in the Middle Ages; up through the early 1600s, it was used to treat any number of Monty Python–type ailments, lumbago and gout. But gin's story—and the decadence it brings with it—doesn't really ramp up until the Colonial era, albeit on the other side of the Atlantic.

As England approached the 1700s, a massive governmental and cultural shift began to take place; at the same time, the American Revolution also began to slowly brew. As the monarchy shifted from Catholic leadership to the Protestant one we know today, all manner of political changes came into play. Among them: Anti-import trade regulations put a nearly impossible tax on imported spirits while simultaneously legalizing the unlicensed production of neutral spirits.

The effects were felt quickly, and they were historical: At the production level, the Crown had allowed distillers big and small to use subpar or even rotten source materials—mainly grain for mash—to produce ever cheaper and more potent varieties of gin. And when that gin went to market, chaos ensued, as the combination of the products' cheapness and the vast impurities it contained created, quite literally, havoc in the streets. This is the Gin Craze of 1720 to

1750, as depicted in William Hogarth's *Gin Lane,* and it is the beginnings of what London readers would later come to know as "Dickensian England."

Although decadence is a slow arc, its instigators live on their own temporal plane. Gin is fast. Gin is mean. And even when it is produced with utmost regard and care, gin can do a number on a body when not consumed in moderation.

And, for the most part, we missed it. The Gin Craze was a uniquely British phenomenon, a product of English politics and tastes. But gin did hit American shores in more humane quantities, and from the word "go," it seemed to intimate the invention of the cocktail:

"At Second and Walnut stood The Three Crowns where one 'scalawag barrister' described a delectable 'flip' that was served:

Into two quarts of old ale (Friend Smith's Brew hath the right Burton smack), pour a half pint of gin, beat four eggs well together with four ounces of sifted sugar. Stir in, little by little, the ale and gin. Then froth by pouring from jug to jug and serve in thin glasses with fresh grated nutmeg on top.

It was common practice to plunge a red-hot poker from the fireplace into a tankard of 'flip' to give it just the right burnt-bitter flavor."

—From *Proper Ale and Pigeon Pye: Tavern Hospitality in Colonial Philadelphia* by Rich Wagner, 2007

In any case, gin would not reach any sort of respectability whatsoever until the 1800s, when the cocktail was finally invented—notably by British soldiers mixing gin with tonic water infused with quinine, given to them by Americans, thereby making it not just a viable prophylactic against malaria but the beginning of a long and beautiful friendship.

VODKA

To behold a glass a of jenever—or "Holland Gin," sold in the United States these days as "genever"—is to sense acutely both the commonalities of human endeavor, as well as the various directions the wind can blow, all at once. Put simply, jenever is a neutral spirit whose distillation can be achieved with either malt or grain, but which is also infused with juniper and can often sometimes taste just like . . . vodka. Primarily made in the Netherlands, it is a kind of crossroads in a glass.

It's also the bridge between gin and vodka, in many ways. And I mention it here not just to parse its flavor profile but to point out that in the seventeenth and eighteenth centuries, this desire for a universal spirit or eau de vie was in fact universal—across a large chunk of the world, at least. From England all the way across Europe and through a Russia whose empire would be consistently shifting for some time to come, a clear spirit in a glass would punctuate times of massive upheaval as, state by state, modernity was being intuited.

In Russia, however, things were a little bit more extreme. The 1600s began with a famine, continued on in a more or less permanent state of war through the 1700s, and along the way, tsars were overthrown constantly as a cultural shift began in the shadows that would land in Russia, by the 1800s, as the home of producers of arts and culture whose influences are still widely felt today.

And it was vodka that got them through it all. (And continues to, to this day.)

Like gin, some version of vodka had been knocking around since antiquity, used primarily as a medicinal. And not just in Russia. Primitive versions of the vodka we know today were common in Poland, Russia, and Sweden. Known alternately as "burn-wine" or "little water"—as well as by the catchall "aqua vitae"—these early vodkas would have been lower in proof and made in smaller batches.

But all that would change in the 1700s, as the first tremors of the Industrial Revolution would begin to sound off. By the middle of the century, Poland would be producing a variety of vodka blends—*Żubrówka*, *Goldwasser*, *Starka*—at industrial distilleries, and in Russia and Poland alike, the spirit became a tool of the state. In Poland, families of the ruling class distilled it almost exclusively, and in Russia, distilling was a fully state-sponsored affair.

But to an early American, where every resource was still hard-won and technology in most cases a distant fantasy, all this would have seemed a world away.

Chapter VIII

From Whiskey to Bourbon

From the very first colonial settlements at Plymouth and Jamestown, one thing became clear: While our intrepid heroes' palates may have been English or Scotch or otherwise continental, America was never going to succeed in and had little desire for rote mimicry of the spirits enjoyed back on the other side of the ocean. Nature saw to it. Their own inventiveness saw to it. And that, really, is what this book is all about.

So let us lock the door of the bar. Pull out the ashtrays for those of us who need them. Let the kitchen staff go, put something decent on the sound system for a change, fetch two tumblers, and consider with me, please, the finality of brown. Whiskey or bourbon or rye, it all pleases the eye. Regard it in the soft light, rocks or neat, and be humbled by its power and complexity. Its dignity. Its unfearing nature and its raw honesty in the face of all the regret to come. It is everything most human beings aren't.

"Whiskey claims to itself alone the exclusive office of sot-making."

—Thomas Jefferson

We owe it all to the Scots and the Irish and . . . corn.

Unlike many of the potables discussed in this time period from the 1600s through the events surrounding American independence, there is actually not a lot of whiskey in colonial America. But like an electrical fire that starts in the walls of a house, the conditions for it are sparking up throughout the entire period. Whiskey in the United States is hampered early on by politics, the competition of rum, plus simple taste and economics. Meanwhile, rum is a monster, a blockbuster, a menace; and ciders, brandies, and ales are as essential and present as daily bread.

But then a few things happen: A greedy monarchy puts the squeeze on the whiskey business in the United Kingdom, sending some of its best distillers scrambling for a place to ply their trade free of hassle or, if we are to be honest, any kind of law and order at all. Farmers and distillers alike find that, though the land is unkind to barley, it is positively laced with corn and rye—especially in Kentucky and Tennessee and Pennsylvania and New York. And finally, capitalism. Capitalism happens as America's newly landed gentry—some of them quite notable, as we shall learn—discover that there is money in whiskey.

And then somewhere in the midst of all this, in the same poor, rocky country that will one day give us American blues and country music, bourbon happens. Bourbon, America's first luxury item. Bourbon, which informs our stance as much as a pair of jeans will one day. Bourbon, which just might be the first thing American men truly owned. Bourbon exists for nearly the same reasons as the United States itself does—in direct defiance of British rule's attempts to control market forces outside of itself wherever possible and tax to the hilt anyone who dared cross its path.

Put this way, bourbon *had* to exist.

Whiskey VS. Bourbon VS. Rye

But before we get ahead of ourselves here, let us answer the question burning in the minds of you, the perhaps novice drinker. What's the difference between bourbon and whiskey and rye?

BOURBON:

mash must be at least 51 percent corn mash
distilled at 160 proof or less
barreled at 125 proof or less
aged in charred-oak barrels
no additives
generally made in the United States, in Kentucky or Tennessee

BY CONTRAST:

WHISKEY:

mash must be at least 51 percent barley
regional, barley-based mash (see Scotch whiskey vs. Irish whiskey)

RYE:

mash must be at least 51 percent rye
popular in the Northeast, commonly western Pennsylvania and Maryland
spicy and less heavy than bourbon

Wee have found a waie to make soe good a drink of Indian corne. I have divers times refused to drinke good strong Englifh beare and choofe to drink that.

—Captain George Thorpe

AMERICAN RYE/ MONONGAHELA RYE & THE WHISKEY REBELLION

Although his origins are patrician in the extreme, Captain George Thorpe's experience is typical of what farmers and distillers would find over and over again during the 1600s and 1700s. Absent the materials and conditions necessary for producing quality English and Irish and Scotch whiskey, not only would corn and rye suffice as source materials, they'd do arguably better than that and stand tall on their own.

Thorpe, in particular, is a patient zero of sorts for American whiskey. A former member of parliament, he was part of a group to whom the Crown awarded a large parcel of land in the mid-1600s near present-day Richmond, Virginia, and was personally charged with establishing all sorts of local resources, business and cultural alike. Among this odd mix was a task near and dear to his heart—converting Native Americans to Christianity—and another one that was much more worthy: setting up a distillery.

What he found in Virginia was that barley was in short supply, but corn was everywhere. So he went with it and found, as noted on page 183, "a waie to make soe good a drink of Indian corne." He runs with it, and so do many, many others. What comes of it all is the beginning of a deeply rooted distilling culture that would only grow in the 1800s.

The South enjoys much of the credit for the development of American whiskey—and yea, bourbon is as deeply Southern as grits—but the establishment of both American booze and its attendant culture comes perhaps just as much out of Ohio, New York, and Pennsylvania. Because once business got rolling, this is where the lion's share of distilleries eventually would be.

Take Monongahela rye, which was synonymous with whiskey during the Colonial era. Named after the river in western Pennsylvania, where the vaguely Irish climate was perfectly suited to the growing of rye, Monongahela rye was sweet and strong. (By contrast, but in direct response to the slightly balmy climate there, Maryland ryes were lighter and more grassy.) Locally produced, strong, and cheap as hell, Monongahela rye became increasingly popular over the years. So popular, in fact, that it generated the foundations of cash needed for the Northeast to slowly but surely approach the industrialization that would characterize the region in the 1800s.

But before all that, there's rye, and the business of rye would continue to grow to the point of toppling anything that got in its way; in 1794, U.S. Marshalls found this out firsthand. When they were sent into the hills of Penn's Woods to collect from distillers and farmers a newly imposed tax on grain spirits, the feds were met with fierce resistance. The Whiskey Rebellion was organized—they had their own flag and platform of regional independence—and impassioned. And, frankly, brazen to the point of frightfulness.

More than five hundred armed men attacked the fortified home of tax inspector General John Neville. Washington—himself in the whiskey business, as we'll discuss in a minute—ordered his army to respond, but by the time they arrived, the rebels had disappeared, thoroughly bedeviling the nascent American state. This type of attack and evasion played out for a while. In the end, distillers simply refused to pay, becoming scofflaws in numbers that stymie the fledgling government authorities. Finally, the whiskey tax was repealed in 1801 after hundreds of men had been charged with violating the law and not much coming of it.

The aftershocks of the Whiskey Rebellion are more important still: The whole affair drove many distillers and their families—many of them Irish and Scotch—to Kentucky, where they got to work on what would become the Bourbon Belt. And even after the potentially reputation-sullying rebellion was over, whiskey in all of its forms was the most popular spirit in the United States after independence and prior to Prohibition.

SPICED WHISKEY

Take of cinnamon, ginger, and coriander seed, each 3 oz.—mace, cloves, and cubels, each, 1½ oz.—Add 11 gallons of proof spirit, and 2 gallons of water, and distil; now tie up 5 oz. of English saffron,—raisins (stoned) 4½ lbs.—dates, 3 do.—liquorice root, 2 do.—Let these stand 12 hours in 2 gallons of water, strain, and add it to the above.—Dulcify the whole with fine sugar.

—From *Five Thousand Receipts in All the Useful and Domestic Arts*
by Colin MacKenzie, 1825

Spiced Whiskey

OUR RECIPE

MAKES ABOUT 1 QUART (960 ML)

For our recipes in this chapter, we have charitably decided not to instruct you to distill your own whiskey. Though potentially fun and profitable, this also would be highly dangerous and deeply illegal. Rather, consider this cocktail, whose flavors might put you in mind of those early days of American whiskey. The cayenne pepper here adds a subtle kick, reminiscent of Atomic Fireball candy. The simple syrup called for is a mixture of equal parts water and granulated sugar with a pinch of salt, heated just until the sugar dissolves; adding it gives the beverage a more liqueur-like feeling.

For more complexity, substitute the simple syrup with a simple syrup made from brown sugar and water, honey and water, maple syrup and water, or a combination of some or all.

12 cinnamon sticks
12 whole cloves
12 allspice berries, cracked
6 cardamom pods, cracked
3 star anise pods

1 (750 ml) bottle whiskey or bourbon
1 vanilla bean, split lengthwise
¼ teaspoon cayenne pepper, optional
½ cup (120 ml) simple syrup, optional,
  see above

- In a small sauté pan, combine the cinnamon sticks, cloves, allspice, cardamom, and star anise and toast over medium-high heat just until fragrant, about 2 minutes.
- Transfer the toasted spices to a 1-quart (960-ml) jar with a tight-fitting lid. Add the whiskey, vanilla bean and seeds, and cayenne papper, if using, to the jar and seal. Store the jar in a cool, dark place for 2 weeks, shaking the jar daily.
- Strain the mixture through a fine-mesh strainer lined with cheesecloth or a couple of coffee filters into a clean container. Add the simple syrup, if using, and store in a tightly sealed jar or bottle. Use within 2 months.

GEORGE WASHINGTON, WHISKEY FOREFATHER

In rural colonial America, then as now, wide gulfs separated farmers, producers/purveyors, and consumers. Today, a dystopian system of agribusiness at the mass-market level controls that market to a degree that some argue whether what the end consumer gets could even qualify as foodstuffs; but back then, the separation was primarily one of class. But don't think it benign: That class distinction filtered down to how spirits came into the world, as well as how they were perceived. Rum brought those issues to the fore, but whiskey did so as well, in different ways.

Consider the series of dilemmas that led none other than George Washington from someone who turned up his nose at corn whiskey to quickly becoming one of America's first liquor magnates. (After he won the Revolutionary War and became our first president, that is.) Upon establishing his estate at Mount Vernon, Washington set about growing tobacco—then synonymous with the idea of cash crops. For a gentleman of Washington's formidable stature, tobacco would have been a natural choice over, say, grain; for sure, that part of the country is still identified with tobacco, where the battered but not beaten cigarette business still plies its trade for national and global markets alike.

But for a savvy creature like Washington, after a time, tobacco became rife with problems. It traded at unstable prices, and Washington had earned the right to like sure things by this point. In addition, tobacco was strongly identified with slavery, which, even in America's first years of independence, had become a highly charged political issue, as well it should have been.

Enter Scotsman James Anderson, who would become Washington's master distiller. Like many others, Anderson came to America explicitly to ply his trade after parliament put the squeeze on Scottish distilleries in order to reduce competition. Having quit the scene in his homeland, he arrived in America—a market, by comparison, that was little regulated and quite thirsty—and found that what the open field lacked in potential for suitable barley it more than made up for in corn and rye. Better still, he happened upon a landlord in George Washington, who, after a bit of thought, was keen on swapping out his tobacco crops for corn.

Washington came around on corn whiskey out of prudence. Barley was not well suited to Virginia's hot climate; corn and rye fared considerably better. Meanwhile, he'd also seen what had happened at Monticello, where his colleague Thomas Jefferson had (as we've seen) great difficulty—which is a more polite way of saying abject failure—in producing wine. The grape may have eluded American vintners, bringing bankruptcy and heartache, but whiskey distillers were determined not to suffer the same fate, and in corn, they found a uniquely abundant and malleable source material.

Jefferson took note and wound up buying a lot of the stuff for his staff and plantation. (Jefferson claimed not to drink "ardent spirits.") But it was Washington who went big. He and Anderson built a stone still house and small malt house on Dogue Creek at Mount Vernon, taking what feels today like a modern, holistic approach: It also had livestock and a mill, with 150 hogs living on leftover corn mash. These were, it turns out, conditions for success.

It's a little-known fact that Washington died as one of America's largest whiskey producers.

MARTHA WASHINGTON'S CHERRY BOUNCE
To Make Excellent Cherry Bounce

Extract the juice of 20 pounds well ripend Morrella cherrys. Add to this 10 quarts of old french brandy and sweeten it with White sugar to your taste. To 5 gallons of this mixture add one ounce of spice such as cinnamon, cloves and nutmegs of each an Equal quantity slightly bruis'd and a pint and half of cherry kirnels that have been gently broken in a mortar. After the liquor has fermented let it stand close-stoped for a month or six weeks then bottle it, remembering to put a lump of Loaf Sugar into each bottle.

—From the memorandum book of Martha Washington

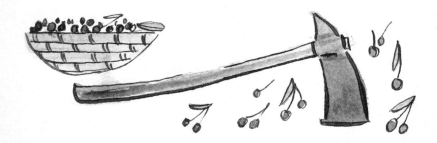

Cherry Bounce

OUR RECIPE

Historically, beverages like this Cherry Bounce would have been used to preserve the flavors of the growing season. And the Washington family themselves were fond of this one. It's meant to be enjoyed around the holidays and throughout winter.

The sugar called for is based on using sour cherries. If you're making it with sweet cherries, reduce the sugar by half and add 2 tablespoons fresh lemon juice. Note the time frame, though, as it's a long one: After 4 to 6 weeks, the Cherry Bounce will be ready to drink; however, flavors will develop more if it's aged 3 to 6 months before straining.

CHERRY BOUNCE
MAKES ABOUT 1 QUART (960 ML)

1 (750 ml) bottle whiskey or bourbon
1 cup (200 g) sugar

1 pound (450 g) sour cherries, stemmed
and pitted
1 vanilla bean, split lengthwise

- In a 1-quart (960-ml) jar with a tight-fitting lid, combine about 1½ cups (360 ml) of the whiskey and the sugar. Seal the jar and shake to dissolve the sugar.
- Add the cherries, vanilla bean and seeds, and the remaining whiskey to the jar and seal again. Shake the jar to combine and then store in a cool, dark place for 4 to 6 weeks (or longer—up to 6 months).
- Strain the mixture through a fine-mesh sieve lined with cheesecloth or a couple of coffee filters into a clean container. Press on the solids to extract as much liquid as possible, then discard the solids.
- Store the mixture in a tightly sealed jar or bottle and use within 2 months.

THE BIRTH OF BOURBON

As the colonies begin to settle and a new wave of Irish and Scottish immigrants rolled in, we finally started to see the beginnings of a liquor industry in what would one day be a free America. Well, "industry" might be a misnomer, because the business was still decidedly crude and homespun. But this is just a piece. Compared to any other options when it comes to spirits, producing corn whiskey was astonishingly cheap and easier than almost anything else—cheapest and easiest of all in Kentucky and Tennessee. As farmers and distillers got to work, the fledgling industry was buoyed and given additional markets thanks to the Ohio and Mississippi Rivers. Both materials and supply went up and down these iconic rivers.

In Kentucky and Tennessee, corn whiskey was born of necessity. There, corn became not just the most viable crop, but in some places, the *only* viable crop. And so corn whiskey quickly outpaced rye—more of a Northern thing—to a degree that is still noticeable in the marketplace today. Along the way, pioneers like Elijah Craig and Jacob Spears innovated using fired barrels—a hand-me-down idea from the rum culture. Taking the process one step further—and borrowing a page from Cognac producers in France—they aged the liquid in said barrels for years at a time.

The result was bourbon. And with this progression, we saw the birth of an entire bourbon culture that still stands today as a core pillar of one flavor of Americana.

The Birth of Bourbon: A Timeline

pre-1763	Kentucky belonged to the French territory of Louisiana, not open to early Americans.
1763	Kentucky becomes part of Virginia and some early settlers (like Daniel Boone) wander in.
1776	Lots of new settlers arrive, mainly Scots-Irish, bringing whiskey-making skills with them.
1780s	Corn-based whiskey is being produced in the eastern and central regions of the territory. All the big names (Evan Williams, Jim Beam, the Samuels family) trace roots back to this period. Five thousand log still houses are operating in Pennsylvania.
1785	Bourbon County, Kentucky, is established.
1789	Elijah Craig begins aging his Kentucky bourbon in charred-oak barrels; he's among the first to do so.
1791	Paris, Kentucky, pioneer and distiller Jacob Spears is said to be the first to name "bourbon." (Story is apocryphal, but notable for its date.)
1801	Whiskey and tobacco officially replace flour as the main export crops from Kentucky's interior (50,000 gallons!).
1810	250,000 gallons!
1822	2,250,000 gallons!!! All of it going down the Mississippi River via the Ohio River, much of it to New Orleans, from where it is spread throughout the South.

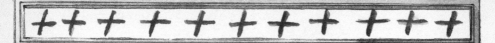

Congeners: It's the Thing that Ails You

With any discussion of whiskey, it'd be lying by omission to not even bring up the topic of congeners. So let's, not just for honesty's sake, but also because that which medically produces the foul beast known as a hangover happens to be a big part of what either is or is not inside of your preferred whiskey.

Early on, Kentucky distillers would sell off a kind of by-product known as congeners. This would have been technically bourbon (emphasis on "technically") that had not seen a charred barrel or the aging process, a bourbon loaded with harsh by-products that either barrels or aging would, in time, kill off. The resulting raw, green spew was as nasty as it gets, and we now know that it literally was a hangover in a glass.

Today, congeners are defined as "substances other than alcohol produced during fermentation. These substances include small amounts of chemicals, such as methanol and other alcohols (known as fusel alcohols), acetone, acetaldehyde, esters, tannins, and aldehydes (e.g., furfural)." In other words, paint thinner. And while it's safe to assume that Colonial-era congeners would have included plenty of proper alcohol too, it's also safe to assume that it still would have been, more or less, paint thinner.

And if you drank it, you'd definitely feel it the next day.

DRINK UP!

What follows here are the classic cocktails that American whiskey and bourbon begat: Your Sazeracs, your old fashioneds, your hot toddys, and your mint juleps. To raise a glass with any of these is to reach back through time so that you might wake up tomorrow morning and wish you were dead.

New Amsterdam
SERVES 1

Named, of course, for the original moniker of old New York, this recipe for a New Amsterdam calls on two of our previous recipes. And it is as dignified a cocktail as you'll find.

2 ounces (60 ml) Cherry Bounce (see recipe, page 191)
½ ounce sweet vermouth
½ ounce dry vermouth

Dash of Orange Bitters (see recipe, page 151)
1 strip (3 x ½ inch/7.5 x 1.5 cm) orange peel, for garnish

In a cocktail shaker full of ice, combine all the ingredients except the orange peel. Shake until chilled and strain into a chilled cocktail glass. Wipe the rim of the glass with the strip of orange peel and garnish.

Sazerac
SERVES 1

The Sazerac—a classic cocktail that has been with us for hundreds of years now and has enjoyed a new popularity in recent years—takes its name from the Sazerac brand of French brandy popular in the 1830s. This recipe, however, presumes that Sazerac and Peychaud's Bitters (also a staple of the classic recipe) had never come into being, using instead the bitters recipes from these pages, and a spot of absinthe as well.

½ ounce absinthe
1 sugar cube
Dash of Raisin Bitters (see recipe, page 165)

Dash of Orange Bitters (see recipe, page 151)
2 ounces (60 ml) whiskey
1 strip orange peel, for garnish

- Fill a rocks glass with ice to chill it. Remove the ice and add the absinthe. Swirl it around the glass to coat the interior. Pour out any remaining absinthe.

- In a cocktail shaker, combine the sugar cube and both bitters and muddle lightly to break up the sugar. Fill the shaker with ice, add the whiskey, and shake until chilled.

- Strain into the absinthe-coated glass and garnish with the strip of orange peel.

MINT JULEP
SERVES 1

Although it is most associated with an iconography of the American South that is decidedly post–Civil War, the mint julep actually traces all the way back to the 1700s, when it was first prescribed as a medicinal. You will see that it hasn't really changed very much. This one uses our Brown Sugar Syrup recipe to roll back the clock a little.

6 mint leaves, plus additional leaves
  for garnish
½ ounce Brown Sugar Syrup
  (see recipe, page 129)

Crushed ice
2 ounces (60 ml) whiskey

In a rocks glass, combine the mint leaves and Brown Sugar Syrup. Muddle to release the flavors of the mint. Fill the glass with crushed ice and pour in the whiskey. Stir to combine and garnish with additional mint leaves.

OLD FASHIONED
SERVES 1

At last, here it is: The first documented "cocktail" in all the world, as noted in the May 6, 1806, issue of *The Balance and Columbian Repository in Hudson, New York*. The recipe has evolved over the years and continues to do so to this day, but ours approximates what would have been on hand at the old fashioned's earliest sighting, using a couple of the recipes we've discussed.

¾ ounce (22 ml) Brown Sugar Syrup
  (see page 129)
3 or 4 dashes of Orange Bitters (see recipe,
  page 151)

2 ounces (60 ml) rye whiskey
Orange twist, for garnish

In a rocks glass, combine the Brown Sugar Syrup and Orange Bitters. Swirl to combine and coat the interior of the glass. Fill the glass halfway with ice and add the rye whiskey. Garnish with the orange twist.

HOT TODDY
SERVES 1

What grog is to rum, the hot toddy is to whiskey. And among all the drinks in this book, it is among the most intuitive in terms of its obvious redeeming powers, that soul-touching goodness when it's cold outside. Here, we've attempted "An Appeal to Heaven," if you will, calling back notes of spruce or rosemary.

2 ounces (60 ml) whiskey
1 tablespoon honey
1 teaspoon dried spruce tips or rosemary

Zest of ½ orange
1 cup (240 ml) boiling water

- In a heatproof mug or container, combine the whiskey and honey. Place the spruce tips and orange zest in a tea infuser (or bundle them in a piece of cheesecloth tied with butcher's twine) and place in the mug or container.
- Pour in the boiling water; cover the mug or container with a small plate or saucer and steep for 5 to 10 minutes. Remove the tea infuser and serve immediately.

WHISKEY SOUR
SERVES 1

This classic, still served in bars all over the world, began its life in the 1700s but would not be put to paper until Jerry Thomas's landmark *The Bartender's Guide* in 1862. Though many bartenders mess around with different spins on the mighty Whiskey Sour, we always fail to see why: Its natural perfection begs everyone to please, please, please just shut up and let us drink in peace.

2 ounces (60 ml) whiskey
1 ounce fresh lemon juice
½ ounce fresh orange juice

½ ounce Brown Sugar Syrup (see recipe, page 129)
Lemon slice, for garnish

In a cocktail shaker full of ice, combine the whiskey, lemon and orange juices, and the syrup and shake until chilled. Strain into a rocks glass full of ice and garnish with the lemon slice.

PEACH COBBLER
SERVES 1

You're thinking of the pie-like dessert, of course. But you are wrong. This is something else.

2 slices ripe peach
1 teaspoon freshly grated peeled ginger
½ ounce fresh lemon juice

½ ounce Peach Syrup (see recipe, page 129)
2 ounces (60 ml) whiskey

In a cocktail shaker, combine the peach slices, ginger, lemon juice, and syrup. Muddle to break up the fruit. Add the whiskey and a little ice and shake until chilled. Pour, unstrained, into a rocks glass and top with more ice if necessary.

CHERRY SMASH
SERVES 1

Predating sodas, but angling for their same sweet appeal, would have been smashes like this one. Using a pair of our earlier recipes, this Cherry Smash, for us, is all about that flourish of thyme at the end. Thyme: Let no man steal it, and certainly do not waste it.

4 to 6 fresh or frozen cherries, pitted
Leaves from a 3-inch (7.5-cm) sprig
*   of thyme, plus 1 spring of thyme*
*   for garnish*

2 ounces (60 ml) Cherry Bounce
*   (see recipe, page 191)*
3 to 4 ounces (90 to 120 ml) Ginger Ale
*   (see recipe, page 137)*

Add the cherries and thyme leaves to a rocks glass and muddle to break up the fruit and bruise the herbs. Add the cherry bounce and stir to combine. Fill the glass with ice and top with the ginger ale; stir gently to blend. Garnish with the thyme sprig.

PUMPKIN SMASH
SERVES 1

Next Christmas, when your brother-in-law goes on about the "bangin'" pumpkin spice ale he tried at the local brewpub, do quietly whip this up for him, serve it with a dunce cap, and request that he drink it in the corner. Thereafter, you may call him Billy Corgan.

2 ounces (60 ml) Spiced Whiskey (see recipe,
*   page 187)*
1 tablespoon pumpkin puree
½ ounce Cinnamon Syrup (see recipe,
*   page 129)*

½ ounce Nutmeg Syrup (see recipe,
*   page 129)*
Soda water
Splash of fresh orange juice
Strip of orange zest, for garnish

In a rocks glass, combine the whiskey, pumpkin puree, and both syrups; stir. Fill the glass with ice, top with soda water and the orange juice, and stir gently to blend. Garnish with the orange zest.

AFTERWORD

One couldn't blame you for quite naturally surmising where this chapter in The Great Story of Booze ends: The Industrial Revolution. As America moved into the 1800s and something recognizable to us today as the earliest days of Big Business began, this colonial era of catch-as-catch-can distilling came to a close. Gone were the days of foraging and making do with whatever was on hand to catch a colonial buzz. Soon, ales, wines, and spirits would be increasingly in the realm of the mercantile and less and less about craft—or, at least, the kind of craft that we'd regard today as distinctly "small batch" and "artisanal." To utter these words in the light of today's trends is only a fraction as disheartening as the actual truth of all of this: When you consider the shift inherent in the industrialization of booze, you can't help but begin to realize that the squeezing of the little guy is almost as old as America itself.

Ah, but once! But once we were free! Once, our forefathers roamed this great countryside, foraging and gathering, eyeing up plants and grains both foreign and familiar, holding them up to an early sun, looking at each other and inquiring, "Hey, ya think you could get stewed on this?"

And the answer was always "yes." Because the question was always about freedom, and ingenuity. Do you think we might find a way to have a good time? Yes. Do you think we might be able to make a buck? Yes. Do you think we might take what we learn, and then learn more and make it better still? Yes.

This book is not meant to be sentimental. These were hard men and unbelievably difficult times: so difficult it is almost impossible for us to understand today. And it's not meant to be simplistic, either. America was founded by people both virtuous and repellent, sometimes down to a man, each individual—signers of the Declaration and poor men alike—capable of both glory and damnation in a single person, in a single day, in a single breath.

But if nothing else, they had a clean slate. They had a glint, a gleaming in the eye, for what they could one day be. And by every account, they had a nearly unquenchable thirst.

We like to think it lives on in us still.

ACKNOWLEDGMENTS

Each day, here in Philadelphia, I walk to and from work, up and down the streets where the very idea of America was hatched. And it is not something I take lightly; to walk these streets, where men like Franklin, Adams, and Jefferson acted with such bravery, both physical and intellectual, is to feel the same electricity of ideas beneath the pavement that once moved their feet. Perhaps that's a bit much for the non–history buff, but over the past years, I've tried to steep my own work in as much history as possible. Because the old saw is true: You can't know where you're going unless you know where you've been.

So it is to the great men and women of early America, the scrappy colonists and ad hoc states-men alike, that I dedicate this book, taking care to point out that I'm not just talking about the big names mentioned above. This book would have been impossible to write were it not for the legends and the recipes and the still-standing frames of America's earliest pubs, taverns, and coffeehouses, the ghosts of which I pass on that same walk every day. Those barkeeps, those tavern-owners, those ne'er-do-wells—this book is entirely about their sense of invention, their irreverence, their common sense in the face of what could have only seemed, at times, like an unreachable summit: If we're going to throw over the Crown, they must have thought, we're going to need a few stiff drinks along the way.

I know that those of us who had a hand in this book often felt the same way, and I owe them a debt of thanks as well. To the Good Reverend and my team at Quaker City Mercantile for their extensive research, exhaustive drinking sessions, and overall help in putting this whole damn thing together—it is to you, and to this great country, still wild and free when it gets out of its own damned way, that I raise this glass. May God bless you all, and may your homes be filled with laughter and a sense of belonging!

The new world belongs to us!

ABOUT THE AUTHOR

STEVEN GRASSE is the renaissance brand maker behind such spirits as Hendrick's Gin, Art in the Age, Narragansett Beer, Sailor Jerry Spiced Rum, and, now, Tamworth Distillery. He started his own firm, Quaker City Mercantile, in 1988, and his work across a wide variety of brands (from MTV to Guinness) and media bears two signature traits: an antic sense of play matched with an equally deep devotion to history. Along the way, Grasse has also applied his renegade spirit to the page; his first book, *The Evil Empire: 101 Ways England Ruined the World*, was a surprise smash to the degree that he still regularly receives calls from the BBC, who'd like to know more.

SELECTED BIBLIOGRAPHY

Baring-Gould, Sabine. *A Book of the West: Being an Introduction to Devon and Cornwall, Volume 2.* Methuen & Co., 1899.

Curtis, Wayne. *And a Bottle of Rum: A History of the World in Ten Cocktails.* New York: Three Rivers Press, 2009.

English, Jason. "Ben Franklin's 200+ Synonyms for 'Drunk.'" In *Pennsylvania Gazette*, January 6, 1737, http://mentalfloss.com/article/29753/ben-franklins-200-synonyms-drunk.

Fry, Joel. "Did John Bartram Introduce rhubarb to North America?" July 20, 2012. https://growinghistory.wordpress.com/2012/07/20/did-john-bartram-introduce-rhubarb-to-north-america.

Gabler, James. *Passions: The Wines and Travels of Thomas Jefferson.* London: Bacchus Pr Ltd, 1995.

George, Rose. "No Bottle: Water," *London Review of Books*, October 8, 2015. www.lrb.co.uk/v36/n24/rose-george/no-bottle.

Graunt, John. *Bills of Mortality.* www.neonatology.org/pdf/graunt.pdf.

Hailman, John. *Thomas Jefferson on Wine.* Jackson, MS: University Press of Mississippi, 2009.

Hucklebridge, Dane. *Bourbon: The History of the American Spirit.* New York: HarperCollins, 2014.

Jacobsen, Rowan. *American Terroir: Savoring the Flavors of Our Woods, Waters, and Fields.* New York: Bloomsbury USA, 2010.

Kemp, Christopher. *Floating Gold: A Natural (and Unnatural) History of Ambergris.* Chicago: University of Chicago Press, 2012.

Kliman, Todd. *The Wild Vine: A Forgotten Grape and the Untold Story of American Wine.* New York: Clarkson Potter, 2010.

Klipps, Robin. "The Art and Mystery of the Apothecary," *The Colonial Williamsburg Foundation*, www.history.org/Foundation/journal/Autumn06/apothecary.cfm.

Leighton, Ann. *Early American Gardens: For Meate or Medicine.* Amherst, MA: University of Massachusetts Press, 1970.

Means, Howard. *Johnny Appleseed: The Man, the Myth, the American Story.* New York: Simon & Schuster, 2012.

Mestel, Rosie. "Snake Oil Salesmen Weren't Always Considered Slimy," *Los Angeles Times*, http://articles.latimes.com/2002/jul/01/health/he-booster1.

Oliver, Garrett. *The Oxford Companion to Beer.* Oxford: Oxford University Press, 2011.

Page, Linda Garland, and **Eliot Wigginton, eds.** *The Foxfire Book of Appalachian Cookery: Regional Memorabilia and Recipes.* New York: Gramercy Books, 1992.

Porter, Henry, and **George Edward Roberts.** *Cups and Their Customs.* London: John Van Voorst, 1869.

Thacher, James, Ezra Collier, and **Allen Danforth.** *The American Orchardist.* Plymouth, MA: Ezra Collier, 1825.

Wagner, Rich. *Proper Ale and Pigeon Pye: Tavern Hospitality in Colonial Philadelphia, Mid-Atlantic Brewing News,* February/March 2007, http://pabreweryhistorians.tripod.com/ MABN0207ColonialTaverns.html.

Washington, George. "To Make Small Beer." *Notebook as a Virginia Colonel,* 1757. The New York Public Library, Manuscripts and Archives Division.

Watson, Ben. *Cider, Hard and Sweet.* Woodstock, VT: Countryman Press, 2013.

Watson's Annals of Philadelphia, Chapter 78: Taverns, www.usgwarchives.net/pa/philadelphia/ watsontoc.htm.

Weaver, William Woys. *Sauerkraut Yankees: Pennsylvania Dutch Foods & Foodways.* 2nd ed. Mechanicsburg, PA: Stackpole Books, 2002.

Wondrich, David. *Imbibe! From Absinthe Cocktail to Whiskey Smash, a Salute in Stories and Drinks to "Professor" Jerry Thomas, Pioneer of the American Bar Featuring the Original Formulae.* New York: Penguin, 2007.

Wondrich, David. *Punch: The Delights (and Dangers) of the Flowing Bowl.* New York: Penguin, 2010.

Wright, Helen S. *Old-Time Recipes for Home Made Wines, Cordials, and Liqueurs.* Boston: Colonial, 1909.

"Alcohol in 1400 to 1600s," Independent Bartending, www.independentbartending.com/ alcohol-in-1400---1600s.html.

"Drug Production in the Seventeenth Century," The National Park Service, www.nps.gov/jame/ learn/historyculture/drug-production-in-the-seventeenth-century.htm.

"The Book of Bourbon," History of Spirits in America, www.discus.org/heritage/spirits/#2.

"30 Days of Thomas Jefferson on Wine," Day14: Final Thoughts, https://drinkwhatyoulike .wordpress.com/2010/09/30/30-days-of-thomas-jefferson-on-wine---the-end.

United States Marine Corps. "History, Customs, and Courtesies," January 1999, www.military training.net/Cpl%20Course/Classes/History%20 107.PDF.

RESOURCES

For Homebrew Supplies:
Conveniently, in our modern world, you can find whatever you require for brewing beer or cider on the Internet—a quick Google search and you're on your way. However, if you're just starting out, we suggest beginning your journey at a local homebrew store. They have not only all of the supplies you need, but also something even more important: expertise. Most brew supply purveyors are more than happy to chat about your beer-related aspirations and can offer the kind of helpful tips and suggestions that come from years of experience.

For Fruits and Vegetables:
Our colonial forefathers only had whatever fresh produce was in season, so we suggest recreating this experience with a trip to your local farmers' market. If you're feeling creative, sign up for a weekly or monthly farm-share or CSA and see what kinds of innovative drinks you can dream up with each delivery. Sweet Potato Cider, anyone?

For Herbs and Spices:
As with produce, most early Americans would have grown or foraged herbs and spices. A small herb garden, either indoors or out, is a gift that keeps on giving for your cocktail creations as well as for food. For more obscure or exotic items, we recommend an online store or a local spice shop—Penn Herb is a local Philadelphia favorite with roots going back to the early twentieth century. (www.pennherb.com)

For Beer, Wine, and Spirits:
The booze world is vast, and there are many local and craft brands popping up every day. In the spirit of the colonists, we encourage you to experiment with using different types and styles of beer, wine, and spirits in this book's recipes. If you're looking for a place to start, we suggest the following fine brands. We can vouch for their quality, and in many cases the flavor profile is not too far from what you might have tasted at the tavern a couple hundred years ago.

BEER
Brown Ale – Dogfish Head Indian Brown Ale
Stout – Founders Breakfast Stout

WINE
Dry Sherry – Taylor Dry Sherry
Ruby Port – Quady Winery Starboard Batch 88
Sparkling Wine – Korbel Chardonnay
Rosé – **Matthiasson Napa Valley Rosé**
Madeira – The Rare Wine Co. Historic Series Madeira: Charleston Sercial Special Reserve

SPIRITS
Gold Rum – Appleton Jamaica Rum Special
Dark Rum – Pusser's Rum
White Rum – Appleton White Jamaica Rum
Brandy – Copper & Kings American Craft Brandy
Peach Brandy – George Washington's Mount Vernon Peach Eau De Vie Brandy
Applejack – Laird & Company Laird's Applejack
Whiskey – Evan Williams White Label
Rye – Rittenhouse Rye
Gin – Gordon's Gin

RECIPE NOTES

RECIPE NOTES

RECIPE NOTES

RECIPE NOTES

Published in 2016 by Abrams Image
An imprint of ABRAMS

Library of Congress Control Number: 2015955674

ISBN: 978-1-4197-2230-1

Editor: Camaren Subhiyah
Designer: Chin-Yee Lai
Production Manager: Anet Sirna-Bruder

The text of this book was composed in Adobe Caslon and Clarendon.

Printed and bound in the United States

10 9 8 7 6 5 4 3 2 1

ABRAMS The Art of Books

115 West 18th Street
New York, NY 10011
www.abramsbooks.com